Praise for *Don't Take No for an Answer*

Les Goldberg admirably proves hard work and dedication is the pathway to success. His unwavering pursuit of quality and success is apparent on every page of Don't Take No for an Answer.
Chuck Whittall
President, Unicorp Companies

With Don't Take No for an Answer, *Les has written master classes on entrepreneurship, leadership, and decency. This book is honest, focused, and, most of all, refreshing. CEOs and those who wish to become CEOs, put this book on your reading list. More leaders should follow his advice.*
Tony Ricotta
Entertainment Executive and
Leadership Consultant

Whether you're just embarking on the entrepreneurial path or taking your business to the next level, Don't Take No for an Answer: Anything is Possible *is a must read. Les Goldberg provides a road map that will guide you toward success. From inspirational to motivational, his real-life stories illustrate why you must never take no for an answer!*
Thank you, Les.
Dr. E. Ann McGee
President, Seminole State College

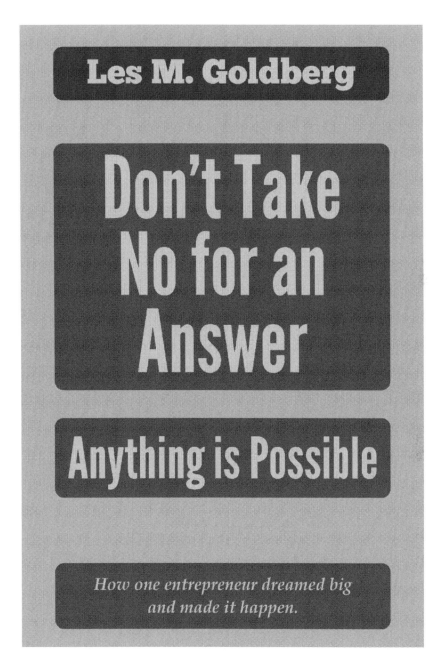

Les M. Goldberg

Don't Take No for an Answer

Anything is Possible

How one entrepreneur dreamed big and made it happen.

Courage to Dream Media
2350 Investors Row
Orlando, FL 32837

This publication is designed to provide accurate and authoritative information in regard to the subject matter covered. It is sold with the understanding that the publisher and author are not engaged in rendering legal, accounting or other professional services. If legal advice or other expert assistance is required, the services of a competent professional person should be sought.

Unless otherwise noted, all photographs are from Les M. Goldberg's personal collection.

Don't Take No for an Answer: Anything is Possible / Les M. Goldberg -- 1st ed.
ISBN 978-0-9963548-0-6

For Grandpa Sam

"The only way to do great work is to love what you do."

—STEVE JOBS

CONTENTS

Foreword

Perhaps it's an overused expression and even cliché to say someone is passionate and driven. We hear that description used for so many and, in reality, most of those people are quite normal in their zest for life and their quest for success.

In the case of Les Goldberg, those words are simply not strong enough.

I was fortunate to meet Les in the early years of his career. He was young and enthusiastic. He had dreams and goals and limited means. He wanted to excel to the highest levels (un)imaginable. For Les, it wasn't so much about the money, but pursuing something about which he was so passionate. Providing quality service with flawless execution surpassed any thoughts of financial success. He knew that to be the best, he would need to render a product that exceeded the expectations of his customers. He couldn't just say he was the best, he had to prove over and over again.

In those early days, his proximity to the Disney property in Orlando offered a true "make or break" scenario for Les and his new company. If he got it right, he would have a business model that could increase year after year. If he got it wrong, it would be tough to reach his ambitious goals.

At that time in his career, I was in a decision-making position at Disney, where flawless vendors were required. Trust and reliability were paramount. Disney was expanding rapidly, so scalability was also critical—vendors had to be able to accommodate the company's growing needs. Already known for quality service in their theme parks, Disney had to get it right if they were to be a world-class convention destination. There were times I would call vendors in the area for specific quantities of equipment, and LMG was the only vendor that offered to take the work. I knew Les didn't always have what we needed in stock, but he said he'd deliver and he always did. Although our business was demanding, in many respects, those were simpler days. As the industry has evolved, it's been fun to watch as Les expanded his operation to provide an ever-increasing range services in multiple locations throughout the country and around the world.

After leaving Disney, I was fortunate to be able to take the great lessons learned there and go on to produce live entertainment and television shows around the world. I have worked on dozens of Oscars and Emmy Award Shows. My work at the Sochi Olympics (my third Olympics) garnered a Telly Award and an Emmy Award Nomination. I have seen excellence at many levels in all parts of the world and Les Goldberg epitomizes excellence. He is among a very small percentage of leaders and visionaries who pursue dreams and create reality.

This book lets you peek into the mind of a true entrepreneur who "gets it." You'll understand how not taking "no" for an answer worked for Les time after time. The advice he shares will help you in your own business operations and even personal relationships.

It's often said that Les has "the Midas touch" because he has been so consistently successful. But, as you'll learn, it's really about strategy. He knows how to recruit the very best people in the business and to keep them happy. He knows how to take a good opportunity and make it great. He knows how to overcome obstacles and recover from setbacks. He knows how to harness passion and to make goals achievable.

This is a remarkable story about a remarkable man. After describing his young start and early lessons he learned through experience, he shares one anecdote after another that clearly and logically provides knowledge that can only be gleaned from 30-plus years of trials, errors, successes, and calculated risk-taking.

I know you will enjoy this book and benefit from knowing Les Goldberg's story.

David Nuckolls
Executive Producer and Director,
Live Shows and Television

Preface

It was a crisp fall day and I was relaxing in comfort on my private jet as I flew across the country to a meeting in Las Vegas, thinking about how all this started. About how a 17-year-old kid with a beat-up Chevy Citation and a projector found something he liked to do that would help him earn some money while he was going to college. About how that kid never understood why something couldn't be done but instead focused on figuring out how to do it. About the successes and setbacks that all worked together to put that kid at the helm of a multimillion-dollar organization that continues to break new ground in the entertainment technology industry.

My tale is the classic American success story. I started with virtually nothing, just a $5,000 loan and an idea that was much bigger than I realized. I used that money to buy a video projector that I rented out for various types of meetings and entertainment events. When I wasn't using it on a job, I stored in my bedroom in my parents' house.

Today LMG has more than 250,000 square feet of warehouse space full of state-of-the-art electronics tracked by a sophisticated inventory management system. Sometimes I look at all the gear and think, "When did I buy all this stuff?" In the beginning, I had one projector and the rental included me as the operator. Today our team consists of hundreds of employees and freelancers who work out of multiple locations across the United States, doing things that we couldn't even have imagined were possible 30 years ago— and they don't let me touch the equipment anymore.

Not long ago, a close friend asked me if what we've built was my plan, if I knew it was going to be like this, if I knew the company was going to grow this big. My answer was: No, I just wanted to do what I loved. It wasn't about size, it was about being the best and building a well-respected organization. That's my definition of success. I wanted to be able to do the Super Bowl, national political conventions, Broadway shows, television productions, and more. The only way to do those is to be big enough to have the resources those events require. So from the company's earliest days, we knew our only option was to grow. But we had to do it smart and we had to do it with distinction. And we had to be agile—we had to respond quickly to advancing technologies, changes in the industry, and needs of our markets.

Over the years, I've watched other audiovisual companies start out strong, be profitable, and then falter and ultimately fail. Still others disappeared as part of corporate acquisitions and industry consolidations. LMG is one of the few that has enjoyed consistent growth and profitability while maintaining its brand identity. Then came the day that I suddenly realized: We were no longer a small company competing against the "big guys"—we *were* a big guy. We had become one of the industry's major players. And there was no way we were going to slow down.

When we reached the point that we needed to adjust our business model so we could continue on our growth trajectory, we created Entertainment Technology Partners (ETP), a technology holding company. We secured funding and made LMG its first acquisition. ETP's purpose is to provide a platform to facilitate growth as its brands take their performance to the next level. We're looking for companies led by like-minded, energetic people who exude passion for what they do. This acquisition strategy is not driven by a goal of aggressive growth but rather by strategic value. We've demonstrated that we know the success formula and the companies that become part of ETP must demonstrate that they know it as well.

In the process of getting to this stage of corporate growth, I realized that when you're running at full speed toward the next goal, the next milestone, you just keep running. You don't look back or even to the sides because that will slow you down. But eventually you get to the point when you can take some time to reflect on a path to success that didn't come easy, that had plenty of failures along the way, but that molded desire, passion, and sheer fortitude into a legacy. This book is that reflection.

Millions of dollars. Thousands of jobs. Shows all over the world. All because way back a geeky kid thought working with audiovisual equipment was fun and he developed a passion for the business that became unstoppable.

My hope is that as you read about our story, you'll find good take-aways that you can apply to your own life and business. But even amid those practical notes, you'll find that our story, as is every success story, one that is driven by a simple concept: You have to be so passionate about what you do that you never take no for an answer because you believe that anything is possible.

Chapter One

Little Les, Big Les, and Early Life Lessons

I've always had a passion for business, for buying and selling things, for figuring out what people want and coming up with a way to deliver it, for negotiating deals, and for being independent. Though I'm not motivated by money specifically, I understood that making money helps you become independent. I think that's why, even as a kid, I liked working and making my own money, especially when I was doing something I enjoyed. I didn't *have* to work; it just never occurred to me not to.

By the time I was 13, I was mowing lawns and doing a combination of after-school jobs and entrepreneurial ventures that appealed to me more because I found them fun to do than for the money I earned. The fact that most of them were also lucrative was a bonus. I briefly tried—and rejected—the common path of youth employment through minimum-wage jobs that required doing things I didn't enjoy. Being in businesses of my choice was just so much more fun. What I didn't realize at the time was how much I was learning—I probably learned the equivalent of an undergraduate degree in business while I was still in high school. And I had no idea I would still be using the lessons I learned as a teenager decades later.

Something else I was fortunate to learn as a teenager was finding out what I wanted to do for a career. That gave me a sense of purpose that not everyone has at that age. In high school, I was the geeky guy who liked working with the audiovisual equipment, running the cameras and projectors, operating the lights, and so on. That experience led to related extracurricular activities and eventually the business I have today.

My family moved from New York to Central Florida when I was a kid. I went to Lake Brantley High School in Altamonte Springs; our mascot was the Patriot. At the time, the school didn't have a video club, so I started one with a couple of friends who were interested in video production. It was perfect timing because back in those days cable companies were mandated by law to produce a certain amount of community programming to maintain their licenses. Storer Cable, one of the independent cable companies serving Central Florida in the early 1980s, was located across from my high school. They figured out that they would meet the community programming requirement by having high school students come in and produce shows. We were free labor and happy to do it for the experience. The video club we started was our entrée into producing a weekly cable show about our school called "Proud to be a Patriot."

We taped shows in Storer's studio. We had a set, we planned the shows, we used the professional equipment, and in the process learned both the technical and the creative side of video production. We produced programs about things going on at the school such as sports and special activities, and those programs aired on Storer's system. It was a tremendous experience and a level of exposure to the business that our little club of teenagers wouldn't have been able to get anywhere else.

One day Betty Fowler, who was in charge of the school's media center, got a call from a local video production company saying they were looking for a gofer, and she knew immediately that I was perfect for the job.

The company was Freedom Television and it was owned by a man named Les White. He was a large man, maybe 350-400 pounds, and they called him Big Les. Of course, that made me Little Les—and it fit, because I was a skinny 14-year-old. Being small worked to my advantage because one of the things I could do was get into the narrow spaces no one else could fit in and run cables. My job included more than just running cables. I was the kid who was willing do whatever you asked, so I would do all the nasty, unpleasant jobs other people refused to do. In addition to creating job security for me, it taught me some valuable things about the production business.

At the time, Big Les ran his company out of his house which, conveniently, was about two streets away from mine. So I could walk or ride my bike to the job, which paid $125 a week for unlimited hours—and I worked as much as I could after school and on weekends. In retrospect, I'm sure Big Les was violating all kinds of labor laws but I didn't care. That job was giving me some excellent experience in the industry that would become my profession and passion. Every day I learned something new and I loved it.

The Lessons Came Early and Often

My first shoot was the Miss National Teenager Pageant. Pat Boone was the host, country star Janie Fricke was there and, of course, all those beautiful teenaged girls—and it was all going to be on national television. The event was held in LeHigh Acres, Florida that year (a four-hour drive from Orlando), which meant it was not just my first location production but also the first time I had gone out of town to work. My parents let me go, and to this day I am still so proud of them for doing that. I'm not sure I would do the same for my kids, especially considering how things went for me on that shoot.

Even though I was just a gofer, Big Les decided to let me run a camera—and the camera was bigger than I was. I was so excited and nervous on the drive down that I couldn't eat.

Shortly after we arrived, I began experiencing stomach pain. We hadn't been on location an hour before the pain was so bad I was lying down in agony. Since I was in too much pain to move, much less work, Big Les took me to the hospital. They notified my parents and my father caught the next flight to Fort Myers, rented a car and drove to the hospital as fast as he could. I can only imagine the panic he and my mom must have felt.

I don't remember exactly what they did for me at the hospital except that they gave me something to eat, the pain went away, and I was fine. And Big Les stood at my bedside and said, "Hell, all I had to do was give you a hamburger." I was cleared to return to work and released from the hospital, and, amazingly enough, my father went home and my parents let me stay for the rest of the production.

Of course, the most obvious lesson I learned from that experience is to remember to eat no matter how hectic things get. But there were plenty more learning opportunities that week. When I returned to the pageant location, they put me on the back center camera, which was a Hitachi SK110. There I was, operating this huge piece of equipment for the first time, with my headset on and the director's voice in my ears telling me to pan left and pan right. The problem was that I didn't know what he meant. The director talked me through it on the headset. He explained that "pan left" meant moving your hands, which are moving the camera lens, to the right and "pan right" meant moving your hands to the left. Even though it was counterintuitive, I'm a quick study; he only had to tell me once. After that, things got easier.

The director was Arie Landrum; he was in his early 50s at the time and had spent most of his life working in television production. To a 14-year-old kid who had to be taught what "pan left" and "pan right" meant, he was very intimidating. But three years later, after Big Les's business was failing and I was freelancing, I found myself working alongside Arie at the 24 Hours of Daytona. He was dumfounded when he saw me. He remembered me from the pageant where he was directing and I was an inexperienced gofer who didn't know how to operate a camera, and there we were, doing the same job as equals at a major sports event. I'd learned a lot in a relatively short period. At Daytona, Arie worked the day shift and I had the night shift as tape ADs. It's one of those jobs that you don't really notice as long as it's done right. Our responsibility was to keep track of how many hours there were in the production, where all the tape playback video segments were, where the sponsor clips were, which machines had what video so we played the right tape at the right time, and so on. It was one of the many things I learned how to do while working for Big Les.

Beyond learning how to operate the equipment in use at the time (which was much larger, heavier, and more cumbersome than today's digital technology), I learned the business side of production. Watching Big Les taught me a lot about what to do and even more about what *not* to do. He wasn't good about paying his bills or keeping his commitments, and he regularly misrepresented his capabilities and tried to make people think his business was bigger and better equipped than it really was. For example, at the time all the big TV networks were using an Ikegami HL79, which was a top-of-the-line camera, one of the first ones that you could put on your shoulder. It was small and very expensive, about $60,000-$70,000 without the lens back then. It had a gray body. Freedom Television had JVC cameras that looked similar but they were orange on the side; they cost about $10,000. Big Les had his employees paint those JVC cameras gray so that from a distance people would think they were Ikegami HL79s—and it wasn't easy to cover bright orange with gray paint. Big Les was also notorious for working his crews long hours with poor equipment and very little guidance. Watching him operate the way he did gave me some of the best business and relationship lessons of my life.

One time Big Les was producing some shows from a golf tournament in Fort Pierce, Florida. It was the Monte Carlo Country Club World Mixed Championship held at what is now known as the Meadowood Golf & Tennis Club; Sam Snead and Joanne Carter won the tournament. These were not live broadcasts; the shows were all prerecorded. Big Les had only done one other similar job and I think he lost money on it, which was probably why he decided to cut some corners on this one. On the first tournament, he rented a real mobile production truck so he could do the live production the right way. For this event, he had a 48' truck that he used to make people think he had a mobile production unit but he never put any equipment in it. It was just an empty truck that we drove down to the tournament—the same kind of tactic he used when he had us paint the JVC cameras. The real production was done in a small RV camper Big Les owned that he named Ethel.

On the first day, before the tournament actually started, we went up in a helicopter to shoot aerials of the course that we could edit into the show later. It was exciting for me then; today, I just shake my head that they would allow a 14-year-old kid to do something like that.

Once the tournament was underway, there were 15 camera operators running around videotaping the action with commentators talking about what was happening. I was paired with Bud Brewer (a well-known sportscaster, talk show host and later public relations executive in Central Florida). We were riding around in a golf cart with Bud recording his commentary and me taping the players. We had to get close enough to do our job and still stay out of the way—and it didn't always work. One time the ball landed in the holder on the back of our cart. Even though I don't remember who the player was, I think he might remember the incident. He had to take a drop and I was trying to hold the camera away from the cart to get it on videotape. I'm sure that footage is lost, but it was the kind of thing that would have gone viral online today.

Throughout the day, our tapes were shuttled back to Ethel where they were edited, then the producer found the best clips and assembled the show. On the first day, Big Les managed to produce a decent one-hour program and got it on the air.

Things didn't go so well on the second day. He was supposed to produce a two-hour program and it just didn't happen. I don't know what all went wrong, but I'm sure it had a lot to do with showing up with an empty truck and trying to produce something without the right equipment. He did manage to put together a half-hour show and the television station had to fill in the rest of the scheduled time with other programming. That taught me a valuable lesson about how much customers count on you when you're doing a live event because there are no do-overs. I later learned that a lot of the people who worked on that tournament and provided equipment never got paid. That pretty much signaled the end for Big Les' company.

> *When you're doing a live event,*
> *customers count on you to do it right the*
> *first time because there are no do-overs.*

There are people who work hard at trying to create the illusion that they're bigger or more important than they really are, and Big Les was obviously one of those people. I think people appreciate honesty more than grand claims. By telling them who you are and what you can do so they can understand what you're good at and what you're not good at, you're giving them the opportunity to make their decision on whether or not to use you based on facts. When you consistently oversell and fall short, you're heading for disaster. But when you undersell and then overwhelm your customers with great service and results, you'll earn their loyalty. They'll not only stick with you, they'll recommend you and help you grow your business.

> *People appreciate honesty more than grand claims.*

While I was working for Big Les, I was at the bottom of the professional food chain. He paid me as little as he could get away with. I got teased, bullied, and pranked. A lot of the guys on Les's crews were in their early 20s—adults, but still immature enough to find humor in doing things like resetting my alarm clock when we were on location shooting a fishing tournament so that I woke up in the middle of the night and was sent running down to the dock in the dark only to find out that we didn't need to be there for another three hours. I got the worst jobs, the things no one else wanted to do, but I didn't care. I would have done anything they asked because I wanted to be part of the group and I was loving the business. I wouldn't trade that experience for anything.

Opportunities for Comparison

When I was in high school, tenth-graders took an aptitude and interest test. It was supposed to tell us what we'd be good at and what would be a good career path for us. My results put television broadcasting at the top of the list. I was already heading down that path with the "Proud to be a Patriot" show at school and working for Big Les. But my job at Freedom Television wasn't the only job I had—I had a number of other jobs and youthful business ventures that gave me real-world experience that classroom instruction alone just can't deliver.

When I was 15, after Big Les' company began falling apart, I worked at a fast food restaurant for about eight weeks. I cooked the burgers and a close friend of mine worked the fry station. But except for my friend, there wasn't anything about that job I enjoyed. Let me stress that there's nothing wrong with working in food service or choosing the restaurant business as a career—it's a multibillion-dollar industry and we have a number of restaurant companies as customers. It just wasn't right for me. I wanted to work doing something that interested me, something I loved. I didn't want to just work for the sake of making money.

Another point to consider is that if making a lot of money is your goal, an entry-level fast food job isn't where you're going to do it. I was working 10-15 hours a week for $3.35 an hour. The restaurant was too far away for me to ride my bike and I was too young to drive, so someone had to take me and pick me up. It was a humbling experience—far more humbling for me than being on the bottom of Big Les's totem pole and a great illustration of why it's important to do work that you love. At the end of my probationary period, the manager congratulated me and told me I was getting a five-cent raise. I did the math: a nickel times 10 or 15 hours. I quit.

That was the last time I worked for anyone else as an

employee. I did a number of interesting short-term freelance gigs including the 1984 Olympics in Los Angeles and the 24 Hours of Daytona race earlier that year, but I had entrepreneurship in my DNA. I'd had several businesses before I was even old enough to drive. The primary thing each of those ventures had in common was the process of figuring out what people wanted and how to be their best source for it—and I loved doing that.

In Business, it Starts with a Sale

When I was in the ninth grade, I was a shy kid. I'm not sure how it happened, but by the time I was in tenth grade, I wasn't shy anymore and I had figured out how much fun it was to sell things. And as the old saying goes, in business, nothing happens until somebody sells something.

I was maybe 14 when I started going to the Maitland Flea Market on Saturday mornings with my friend Keith Quilty. My mom would get up and drive us. We'd get there early, usually by six or six-thirty in the morning, with no merchandise and $50 each in our pockets. As other sellers arrived and started unloading, we'd hang around their cars, helping them unload and trying to buy their stuff. It was classic: They'd say, "I want $10 for this." Keith or I would say, "I'll give you $5." Sometimes they took our offer because they just wanted to sell what they had and get out of there, sometimes they turned us down. Enough of our offers were accepted that by eight o'clock, we'd have a whole table full of things we could sell at double or more what we paid. And by the time the market closed for the day, we would have sold everything. It was a great way for a couple of enterprising kids to spend their Saturdays.

When FleaWorld (which billed itself as the world's largest flea market) opened in Sanford, Florida, we were there on the first day. It was a Thursday, so we couldn't go until after school. We'd just bought the contents of a little warehouse from a guy who wanted to get rid of it and was willing to sell everything to us at a discount—everything in a double storage unit for $400. It wasn't all junk; there was some good stuff in there. In fact, I paid Keith $100 because I wanted to keep some of it.

Keith borrowed his father's car and we crammed it as full as we could and headed to the new flea market. The only people there were other dealers and those dealers bought everything we had. Picture it: on this huge new flea market's opening day, we were the most successful seller—two kids who had to go to school first, and I wasn't even old enough to drive. We had the best day and we were there less than two hours. We still laugh about that today.

I didn't limit my buying and selling to flea markets. We went to garage sales and auctions to buy and we sold wherever there was an opportunity. I even sold things at school. I didn't have one of those cartoon-style jackets lined with pockets that I could open to be a walking display case, but I always had something to sell and people knew they could come to me for a good deal. I sold towels to the athletic department, socket sets to other students, and all kinds of inexpensive imported goods.

Another one of my early business ventures was called Youth Marketing Services. It was a fancy name for a simple operation—I and some friends would deliver flyers around neighborhoods on our bicycles. I was 15, and it was my first experience with having "employees" because I would negotiate the deal with the advertiser then recruit and pay other kids to help me with the distribution.

My final high school business venture occurred on graduation day. These days, it's standard practice to create professional and amateur videos of important (and not-so-important) life events. But when I graduated from high school in 1984, it wasn't a common thing—not everyone had a video camera. It occurred to me that some of the parents of my classmates might buy a video of the graduation ceremony, so I set up a camera and hired someone else to operate it while I walked. Then I sold VHS copies to the parents.

By the way, we recently discovered that original tape and, with a great deal of TLC, our technicians were able to transfer it to DVD. If you were a 1984 graduate of Lake Brantley, I'd be happy to send you a copy of the DVD.

With high school and graduation out of the way, it was time to make some decisions. I knew I loved business. I loved selling. And I loved the production industry. But I was still only 17 and my parents wanted me to go to college. I did the only thing I could figure out to do: Everything.

Chapter Two

Getting it Started

In early 1984, I got the idea for the business that would become LMG. I was 17, I had finished high school (I completed my required credits in December 1983, although I wouldn't officially graduate until June) and I was looking for a way to earn money while I was going to college.

At the time, Orlando's convention industry was starting to boom and closed-circuit satellite events were growing in popularity. Remember, this was long before live internet streaming was available. Promoters would make their events (typically live boxing matches but sometimes other types of events) available on a satellite feed. The venues (bars, restaurants, hotels, etc.) would pay a fee to access the feed, show the event on a big screen in their facility using a rented projector and freelancer operator, and charge admission. It was a great revenue stream for the venues as well as the promoters.

While I was working for Freedom Television, I learned how to operate an Aquastar projector. It was one of the first video projectors with three guns (red, green and blue)— definitely primitive by today's standards, but cutting edge back then. The audiovisual companies in the area at the time had not invested in this type of projector; they were more focused on slide projection rather than video. I told my dad I was thinking about buying an Aquastar because no one else was offering them. I thought there would be a good rental market for them and it would be a good way for me to generate income while I was in college.

The projectors cost about $15,000 new; my dad suggested looking for a used one. It took some time and effort (remember, this was before the internet) but in late February I found one for sale by a company in New York for $4,500. I lined up the deal with Barry Bernstein of Video Techniques; he told me he was coming to Florida in a few weeks and would bring the projector with him. We agreed to meet at the Orlando Airport Marriott on March 17 to complete the deal.

When I told my dad, he said, "Before you buy it, why don't you call ten people and just ask them if they'd use it?"It was market research at its most basic and it made sense. So I got on the phone.

One of the people I called was Tom Amason, a hotel AV manager I had met while working for Big Les. I wasn't sure if he even knew my name. I said, "Hey, Tom, do you remember me? Les Goldberg. I've been in the hotel once or twice doing a show with a satellite dish." He said he remembered me, so I continued: "I'm on my own now and I'm thinking about buying an Aquastar projector to rent out. I wanted to know if it's something you think you might be able to use."

"Definitely," he said. Before I could say "thanks" and end the call, he surprised me. He added, "I need it for March 17."

I wanted to be sure I'd heard him correctly. "March 17? What time, Tom?"

"Two o'clock."

I did some rapid calculations in my head. I was scheduled to pick up the projector up at noon at the airport and would need enough time to complete the transaction and then drive to Tom's site.

"We can do that," I said confidently.

Then he asked how much I charged. Of course, I hadn't thought about that, but I didn't see any reason to say so. I picked a number that I thought sounded good. "It's $400 and includes me for 10 hours," I said. Tom agreed.

On March 17, Barry Bernstein met me in a hallway of the Orlando Airport Marriott. We took the projector out of the box, plugged it in, and it worked. I paid him $4,500 and headed off to Tom's hotel.

And that was my first booking. I've never forgotten it, and I've always appreciated Tom's faith in me. In fact, I called him on LMG's 30th anniversary to thank him. That first Aquastar projector and screen are long gone, but we still have the road case for the projector. I bought it for $318 from a guy who still freelances with us today, and we have it on display in our headquarters building with a plaque on it that says "Road Case 1."

I was an enterprising kid, but I didn't have the cash to pay for the projector. My grandfather loaned me $5,000 so I was able to buy the projector and get a 9'x12' screen. I paid him back at 10 percent interest over three years. In actual dollars, his return on that investment wasn't a big deal for him but his willingness to take a chance on my idea provided a return for me far greater than either one of us could have dreamed of at the time.

Going from Idea to Serious Business

One of those initial phone calls I made to determine if there was indeed a market for what I wanted to do was to a guy in New York who asked the name of my company. After a brief pause (I did a lot of fast thinking on those calls), I said, "LMG," my initials. It just popped out. And the name stuck. If I had taken some time to consider it, I might have come up with something more clever or reflective of what I was doing, but the name worked then and continues to work today.

That simple idea to make money while I was in college—buy a projector and rent it out for $400 a day—went from concept in February to one rental in March to nineteen rentals in October. That was almost more than I could handle and a few times I had to pay someone to cover for me on the job while I was in class. What's more, my equipment inventory was growing because once I started getting jobs and people liked what I did, they began calling me for bigger projects that required more equipment. I was putting everything I made after expenses back into the business, building my inventory so I could do bigger and better shows.

It wasn't long before I needed an office with a legitimate business address and a place for all the equipment I was accumulating. I was still living at home with my parents and my inventory had spilled out of my bedroom into the garage and bonus room. I found a one-room office and furnished it with a small desk and chair. That lasted about six months before I had to move into a warehouse.

I was still a small operation, functioning as a sole proprietor, but I had employees and inventory and was making money. It was time to form a business entity.

To do that, I needed an attorney, so I opened up the telephone directory (remember, this was 1984 when people still let their "fingers do the walking through the Yellow Pages") and started looking for someone near me. I found Harvey Alper, an attorney whose office was a short drive from mine. I called and explained that I was 17 and wanted to form a corporation, and asked if he could help me with the paperwork. He thought one of his associates was playing a joke on him, so he said, "Sure, come on down." He was surprised when I actually walked through the door a few minutes later, but he treated me with respect and did the paperwork for me. He still represents me on some legal matters today.

During those first few years, LMG occupied several

different commercial spaces on the north side of Orlando, moving to larger facilities as we continued to grow and accumulate inventory. The offices were close to my parents' home and the campus of Seminole State College because I was still living with them and going to school. But we were on the other side of the metro area from most of our job sites, which were near what we call the attractions area and the Orange County Convention Center. When we found ourselves again outgrowing our space for the sixth time, we decided it was time to move our operation closer to where our customers were. And instead of renting, we would buy land and build.

It was a bold decision for someone not long out of his teens.

Buying Land, Building a Facility

I went shopping for real estate and found one acre on Presidents Drive in Orlando Central Park, which at the time was owned by Lockheed Martin. They were asking $180,000 and I told them they needed to sell that land to me for $120,000. I said, "This is good for you because you don't have any other 24-year-olds buying land and I'm good for the community." I thought it sounded impressive, even if I wasn't sure exactly what I meant. I don't know if they agreed with me or if they were just amused by me or if they simply wanted to get rid of the land and it wasn't that big of a deal for them, but they accepted my offer. My mom was a Realtor and she drew up the purchase contract for me.

The next step was to apply for a loan; I went to a bank and got raked over the coals. They soaked me with all kinds of fees and charges that I would never pay today—in fact, no bank I deal with now would even try to do what they did to me then. But at the time, it was the only way I could get the money. In fact, when I asked about all the fees, the banker said, "Look, you need the bank more than the bank needs you right now, so you're going to pay the fees." It was another valuable lesson learned early: I had to grow my company big enough so that our business would make a difference to the bank, and when we reached that point, we'd get better terms.

With the land deal done, it was time to design and build a facility. The space I was renting at the time was owned by a construction company, so my landlords ultimately built my first building. It was 14,000 square feet and we thought it would be so big that we could put a racquetball court in it. We didn't do that—we were too busy working and growing the company to the point that we ran out of room and had to store equipment in other locations.

It was a very proud day when we moved into that first building. We were only eight years old with 25 employees and this new fantastic building that we owned. And it wasn't long before we realized that we needed more space again.

In 1994, we began looking around for land for another building. We were expanding, making plenty of money, and had some ambitious plans. We decided to build a little bigger than we thought we could afford, but we believed that was a good long-term strategy, and we were right. We moved into the new building (the one we're in now) in 1996.

Here's an amusing side note: When we put the old building on the market, we got an offer under a blind buyer contract. It turned out the buyer was one of our competitors who thought we'd refuse to sell to them if we knew who they were. While it's true that we're in a competitive business, I believe in competing on performance, on the value LMG brings to the table for the customer. I didn't care who bought the building as long as they paid the price, and I thought it was comical that they insisted on locking in the deal before they revealed their identity. They were eventually acquired by a bigger company; it's somewhat ironic that we didn't know who they were then, and now no one does.

Not long after we moved into the new building the economy slowed substantially due to the dot-com bust—something we could not have foreseen. We had some "what have we done!" moments, but we stayed on our growth path. Eventually it was time to expand our headquarters facility again. We were considering sites when a friend of mine told me there was a way we could buy and develop the designated wetlands that were next to our existing building. It wasn't a simple process, but it was still easier than building from the ground up again and moving.

Orlando Central Park was willing to sell me the land at wetlands prices, which were a fraction of the cost of shovel-ready land. In 1995 I bought the first five acres we're on for $625,000. Just a decade or so later, I paid $99,000 for six adjacent acres. Then I bought environmental credits that would be used to purchase and preserve other wetlands. Once we were approved to build, we had to do a substantial amount of prep work to get the wetlands dug out, refilled, and ready for construction. After jumping through a lot of hoops, our headquarters building was expanded to 105,000 square feet and contains one of the largest air-conditioned staging facilities in the United States—and it's going to get larger. We're ready to expand the headquarters building to 155,000 square feet. That our warehouse is air conditioned is important—it's something that not all of the players in our industry have and it makes LMG a desirable place to work because our people are comfortable year-round. It's just one more thing we've done to attract top talent.

During that time, we were doing more than just expanding our Orlando office, we were growing nationally. Today, in addition to our facility in the Orange County Convention Center, we have operations in Las Vegas, Dallas, Tampa, Nashville and Detroit. I own our headquarters building and the custom-designed 64,000-square-foot Las Vegas facility.

There are differing schools of thought when it comes to owning your own facilities. One is that the real estate is an appreciating asset and you have more control as an owner. Another is that when you own a building, you're stuck with it. If you're forced to work inefficiently because the building isn't the right size or configuration for your operation, your growth might be hampered. Both perspectives are valid.

What owning buildings brought us was legitimacy,

credibility, and a significant strategic advantage. But it's more than simply owning the property. The size and design of our headquarters facility makes a powerful statement. It impresses our customers, intimidates our competitors, and helps us attract top talent because it's a great working environment. It shows everyone that we're a substantial company and we're here for the long-term.

Knowing Who We Are

It's one thing to say that we provide creative technical solutions for events—while that's what we do, it doesn't say who we are. To do that, we needed to articulate our vision, mission, and core values. This is a valuable exercise which should be done as early as possible in the development of any company.

Our Vision

To build relationships and deliver extraordinary experiences through technology and imagination.

Our Mission

To go beyond technology as a global leader by introducing innovative solutions you can trust, through a distinctive approach to quality, service, and support. We seek to develop lasting relationships with our customers, partners, and employees under the highest ethical and professional standards. We are committed to diversity, safety, and professional growth with our pledge to excellence.

Our Values

Passion

Inspired to go the extra mile with pride and enthusiasm

Relationships

Cultivating connections with friends, colleagues and clients with mutual respect

Teamwork

Working together while directing individual accomplishments toward achieving company goals

Professionalism

Treating others courteously and communicating respectfully

Continuous Improvement

Advancing knowledge, sharpening skills and trying new ways to provide better service

We share this with our customers, our suppliers, and, of course, our employees and freelancers. While I might not have expressed these values in the same words in those early days, they have been the guiding principles for LMG from the beginning.

Growing the People Side of the Company

Before I started LMG, I was working as a freelancer in the production field. I was essentially a warm body that knew how to operate someone else's equipment. When I started the company, I stepped up to being a freelancer with my own equipment (a projector)—it was just me going out on contract jobs at first. But it wasn't long before I needed help and had to start hiring people. As I've mentioned, this wasn't my first time as an employer; I had hired friends to work for Youth Marketing Services, a company I had when I was in middle school. But with LMG the stakes were higher for everyone. Customers were counting on us to show up at their events and do the job right. The people I hired depended on me to train them, provide the work, and pay them on schedule. Because I had made a substantial (for me at the time) investment in equipment, I needed to generate revenue. And my reputation was on the line—I was young and didn't have a lot of experience, but I knew even then how important your reputation is and that the people I hired reflected on me.

> *Hiring the right people—people who share your values and commitment to performance—is essential to your success.*

During those early years, everybody reported to me directly. We were a fairly typical start-up: As the owner, I was involved in everything and handled most of the sales and general management responsibilities. About the time we hit 25 employees, I knew we had to add middle management if we were going to continue to grow. That was more challenging than I expected, which I'll explain in Chapter 5.

We went through some interesting staffing evolutions over the years. Not all of the people who were a fit when we were just getting started were right for the company after we hit the $1 million mark. We needed different skills to reach the $10 million level. And when we were closing in on $25 million, I had to bring in new people who had the aptitude to take the company past that milestone.

I've always believed I should treat people like I wanted to be treated so that's the approach I take to hiring and managing. Some of what I learned about the process came from doing things right. Some came from making mistakes. And a lot came from taking advantage of the business I was in. By providing support for the meeting industry, and in particular by renting and operating teleprompters and supplying other equipment that required me to be in the room during all kinds of meetings, I've had the opportunity to sit through more than a thousand presentations featuring experts of all kinds explaining how to do things better. I've heard speakers ranging from the newest expert on a particular subject to the most respected motivational speakers and even all of the living Presidents since Jimmy Carter—people who charge tens of thousands and even hundreds of thousands of dollars for their appearances. I've seen every type of speaker and every type of delivery—the people who hold on to the lectern for dear life and read the teleprompter word for word and the people who bounce all over the stage and don't read the script at all. It was a phenomenal education. I learned from them and applied that knowledge to LMG.

Chapter Three

Setting Priorities, Getting Things Done

We all have a finite amount of time on this earth. We can use that time wisely or we can squander it. Part of using time wisely means knowing how to make good decisions when it comes to setting priorities and getting things done.

Good habits are an essential ingredient for success, and the earlier you develop good habits, the better. Get in the habit of doing things that are good for you as an individual and for your business. When doing things that are good for you physically and spiritually are so much a part of your routine that they are second-nature, you'll be healthier and happier. The same applies to business habits; practice doing things that are good for your business until they become automatic. Integrating good habits into your overall lifestyle—business and personal—increases your efficiency and effectiveness. And when circumstances arise that are outside the norm, it will be easier for you to focus your energy on dealing with those issues. Good habits set you on the right course and let you put handling day-to-day matters almost on autopilot.

We live in a world that's full of distractions. Good habits such as eating right, exercising, and avoiding excess in all areas help develop your mental acuity and keep your brain focused on what you need to accomplish. Good habits and discipline go hand-in-hand. I think of discipline as doing what you should do because you know you should do it. It's knowing when to say yes and when to say no. And it's also knowing when it's okay to indulge in something you might not ordinarily do.

I don't think I could have articulated this as a teenager or even in my early 20s, but I practiced it even without realizing it. I was dedicated to my business and worked long hours, but I still had friends and a social life (balance and moderation are good habits, in my opinion). I intuitively understood that if I developed good habits, worked hard, and made some sacrifices in those early days I would see a payoff later.

Going for the Gold

After I finished high school (as I mentioned, I completed my course requirements in December but didn't actually graduate until the following June), I got several gigs as a grip at broadcast events at the Daytona International Speedway. I got paid $75 a day (not bad for a 17-year-old in 1984) and did whatever needed to be done. During a motorcycle race, I was sent out to pit row with a camera operator; my job was to hold the little microwave antennae that would transmit what he was shooting. The motorcycles were coming fast and close on either side of us, and it was scary. I didn't find it particularly comforting when I heard the director say, "Don't worry, I've never lost any cameramen." He didn't say anything about not having lost any grips who were holding the antenna.

A few weeks later, I was working the 24 Hours of Daytona (a sports car endurance race) and had the opportunity to meet the legendary Fred Rheinstein, a postproduction industry pioneer and founder of The Post Group. Motorweek Productions, another one of Fred's ventures, was doing live racing coverage. Joel Westbrook, the production manager for Motorweek, asked me to thread some tape machines to see if I knew how to do it. When I showed him that I did, he said casually, "I might be able to use you in LA for the Olympics." That nonchalant remark was like a shot of adrenaline. I wanted that gig! Later Joel invited me to fly out to California for an interview. The timing meant missing my senior prom, but I thought it was worth it. And I was proved right when they called me a few weeks later to offer me the job. I was 17 years old, just out of high school, and working on the production team of the world's premier athletic competition.

One of my sisters lived in Van Nuys at the time, just 15 minutes away from the Production Group's studio in Hollywood. I was able to stay with her, but I needed transportation to get to and from the job. At 17, I couldn't rent a car from a traditional car rental company, so I found a buy here, pay here used car lot and the owner was willing to let me rent a Ford Grenada for $100 a day for 20 days. It was a steep price, but I was earning $450 a day, so I could afford it. Even though he was overcharging me and probably not following any of the usual rules for car rentals, I didn't care—I had transportation, the car was insured, and that was all I needed.

The day before pre-production was scheduled to start, I showed up to learn how to use the equipment. They sat me down in front of a piece of equipment called an ADDA, a still image storage device that I wasn't familiar with, and handed me the manual. Fred walked in, saw me, and said in his nicest terms, "Les, we didn't want to fly you in, but now that you're here, don't f*** up!" And he walked out.

I don't know if I was even breathing. I know my hands were frozen to the arms of the chair. I finally took a breath, read the book, and figured out the machine. The only problem at that point was that the crew I was on was doing the broadcast for Mexico and everything was in Spanish. I didn't speak a word of Spanish and neither did several other crew members. It was tough for us to do our jobs when we didn't know what was going on. We were frustrated, trying hard but having trouble communicating, when one of the guys told a joke in English and someone who we thought couldn't speak English started laughing. Turned out he was bilingual, so he took over as our translator and things got easier.

I'd been there several days when Joel Westbrook asked me how old I was. At first, I wouldn't answer. He pressed me, saying, "It's not going to change anything, I just need to know." I finally confessed to being 17, and he said, "We don't even look at resumes from 17-year-olds!" I just said, "Well, I'm here." It was a good thing for me that it hadn't occurred to him to find out how old I was when we first met in Daytona.

It didn't take me long to realize that if you present yourself well, have an air of confidence, and know what you're talking about, people will take you seriously no matter how old you are. And if you get rattled, the key is to not let anyone know it. For example, I was just 20 years old when I was working at a conference at Miami Beach's famous Fontainebleau Hotel where sex therapist Dr. Ruth Westheimer was speaking to a meeting of Hadassah, the Women's Zionist Organization of America, which is part of an international Jewish volunteer women's organization. I was accustomed to listening to and learning from the speakers when I worked at events, but Dr. Ruth was speaking to these women about orgasms. To say this took me out of my comfort zone was the understatement of the decade. But I kept my feelings to myself and just did my job. Then there was the time we were doing a satellite downlink at the former

Sheraton Twin Towers (now a Doubletree) in Orlando; the audience was there to see an internationally-known preacher. But one side of the satellite was set to receive religious programming and the other side was porn. And—you guessed it—someone had flipped the switch to the wrong channel. When these things happen, you don't freak out, you just stay calm and fix them.

Overnight Riches Take Years

I know a lot of successful people and not even one of them made their fortune overnight like they won the lottery. Unless it's inherited, wealth is usually acquired through hard work over a period of time. It could take 10 to 20 years before you start seeing a personal economic payoff for the effort you put into your business.

We live in a culture of instant gratification. In particular, the GenXers and Millennials (but this even applies to some Boomers) want immediate results. They want to build a million-dollar business in a weekend and have the money roll in while they're out playing. It doesn't work that way. Creating and growing a profitable company takes hard work. It takes the proverbial blood, sweat, and tears. It takes commitment. Most important, it takes time. And that's why the business you choose needs to be something you love and are passionate about.

> *Creating and growing a profitable company takes hard work. It takes the proverbial blood, sweat, and tears. It takes commitment. Most important, it takes time.*

When I started LMG more than three decades ago, it wasn't with the goal of getting rich. I just wanted a way to earn money while I was in college and I wanted to be doing something I loved. It happened that the idea I came up with at the time turned out to be viable for a long-term business that has been successful and consistently profitable. But building my own personal wealth was never a priority or even a primary motivator for me—and if you want to be truly successful, it shouldn't be for you.

When I speak to young people, when I look at advertisements targeted to investors and would-be entrepreneurs, it seems like everyone just wants to be rich. What's important to understand is that wealth is the result of something. You can't just say "I'd like to be rich," sign the form, and—poof!—you're rich. Wealth is a derivative of hard work and of being the best at what you do. It's not a realistic short-term goal. And short-term thinking is the wrong approach for an entrepreneur who wants to be successful.

Spend Where it Counts, When it Counts

You've probably heard the traditional "fake it 'til you make it" advice that suggests you do your best to look the part of being successful even if you're not there yet. I think a better strategy is to focus on truly making it so you don't have to fake anything. And once you make it, you don't have to worry about looking the part.

A case in point: My first car was an old Chevy Citation. I bought it when I was in high school. It leaked oil and made weird noises, but it had a hatchback and I could fit my projector in it. I might have kept that car all the way through college but my parents gave me a Chrysler Laser as a high school graduation gift. That car was very cool; it even talked ("your door is ajar"). But I wouldn't have bought it for myself at the time. I preferred to spend the money I was making on more equipment for the company so the company could grow.

That was the approach I used for years. When it came to making the choice between buying something for myself or buying something for the business, my personal wants were not in first or second position—I came in last. If paying my employees meant I couldn't pay myself, that was just part of the deal. Back then I didn't have access to unlimited funds or a private plane or a network of influential people who would take my calls. But I have those things today (well, the funds aren't literally unlimited, but I have the resources to accomplish my short- and long-term goals) because my priority was building my business on a solid foundation that would last.

Building a Track Record when You Don't Have One

One of the biggest challenges of being a new business or expanding a business into a new market is proving you can do the work when you don't have much of a track record. That's where relationships come in.

Though I didn't consciously understand the full value of relationships when I started LMG, I figured it out early on. When I was doing my preliminary market research to decide if I should buy that first projector, and then later after I had it, many of the prospective customers I contacted were people I'd met and established a connection with while I was working for Freedom Television. I quickly realized that what counted was not just knowing people, it was having relationships with them. In a business context, this meant that they trusted me and believed that I would do what I promised. In return, I made sure that they knew I was genuinely committed to their success and to doing whatever it took to meet their needs—and then some.

Back then, the internet and the ability to build websites that could create the illusion of size didn't exist. LMG was a small company and, like most small companies, we were capital-constrained. What money we had was invested in equipment. We didn't have money to spend on superficial things like fancy brochures, expensive entertainment, and other trappings designed to impress customers and create the illusion that we were a big company. It was all about delivering what we promised and more, and building trust and relationships through superior performance. When you're focused taking care of customers, you do things because they're right, because you know they'll strengthen the relationship, not because they'll make you money.

From the very beginning, customers chose LMG because we had a relationship. They knew me, they trusted me, and when I said I could and would do something, I delivered. I was in it for the long-term and they knew it. Equally important is that the relationships went both ways. Just as the customers trusted me to do what I promised, I trusted them to be honest with me and pay me when the job was done. As the company grew, those relationships expanded beyond me to the rest of the team—it wasn't just Les Goldberg anymore, it's the company and everyone who works with us.

Today when we pitch a new customer, we can point to more than 30 years of experience, an equipment inventory worth millions of dollars, and tens of thousands of successful shows. In those early days, before we had this track record, the business was built on trust and relationships, and that remains the foundation of our operation today. As the company grew and we expanded our offerings, our relationships gave us leverage. Our existing customers were willing to give us a chance with bigger and better projects, because we had a relationship and credibility.

It always helps to have experience and a track record. It's great when you can honestly say, "We did this for someone else, we can do it for you." When your business is new or when you're launching a new product or service, you can't always do that. But if you have built solid relationships, you'll find people willing to give you a shot because they trust you.

Investing in a relationship is the key to producing something from it. It works in marriage, it works with family and friends, and it works in business. If you're not willing to invest, you're not likely to get dividends.

Regardless of whether you're a start-up or an established company, or how big or small you are, the most effective way to prove yourself and build your track record is to be the very best at what you do.

Making Magic

LMG had only been in business a couple of years when we started doing work for Disney. This was back in the mid-1980s and Disney was like a different company—they didn't have all the hotels they have now and their convention segment wasn't anywhere near as sophisticated as it is today. One of the things we provided for Disney back then was teleprompters, which means we (and that was mostly me at the time) had access to the scripts and speeches for the conventions and meetings. We were so involved in their presentations that the Disney culture became ingrained in us. It's a culture of customer service, empowering employees, protecting the brand, and doing the right thing because it's the right thing.

Another bit of culture we acquired from working with Disney in those early days is twofold: As a supplier, we do whatever it takes to meet the customer's needs and as a customer, we take care of our suppliers. Here's an example of that: A large group was staying at Disney's Dolphin Hotel and they wanted baby monitors in their rooms. The hotel didn't have any, so management asked the AV office for help, and the AV office called me. There wasn't time to negotiate anything. I just asked how many, went out and found the baby monitors, delivered them to the hotel, and submitted my bill. I knew I would get paid. I took care of them and they took care of me. Now, I don't recommend doing every transaction this way. Written agreements are an important part of business. But when you have a relationship built on trust and you don't have time to hammer out a contract, you just get it done.

More than Perseverance

The old saying, "If at first you don't succeed, try, try again" is only partially right. Certainly you should try again—but not before you take the time to figure out what you need to do differently to win. If you go to battle and you lose, and you don't learn from it, then you're not smart. And all the perseverance in the world won't help if you're doing it wrong.

> *If you go to battle and you lose, be sure you learn from it so you know what to do differently next time.*

We have been the onsite provider of audiovisual services for the Orange County [Florida] Convention Center (OCCC) since 1999. The first time we bid on the contract, we lost— and it was one of the most valuable lessons we ever learned.

We put our heart and soul into that first bid, but we hadn't bid on a convention center contract before and there were some things about the process that we didn't understand. One key issue was that the contract was evaluated on a point system. After the contract was awarded to another company, we invested the time necessary to figure out where our low scores were and what we had to do to improve them. The next time the contract was put out for bid, we won.

When you're working within a bid system, especially with a government or quasi-government agency, it's essential that you understand what the customer needs to know and that you organize your bid in a way that answers their questions in a clear, organized way. This was another lesson we learned the hard way. After we had been the onsite provider for several years, the contract was put out for bid, which is standard operating procedure for the OCCC. We knew we'd been doing an excellent job and the bid we submitted that time was even better than our first winning effort, but to our complete and utter shock, we lost. The reason was not because the other proposal was better, it was because the scoring committee missed some critical information in our bid. That taught us the importance of making sure our bids are well-organized and easy to navigate so that readers can easily find and properly evaluate the information. It also reinforced something we already knew: When you lose a bid, find out why and what you could have done differently. You'll find that customers are often willing to give you feedback on your proposal even after they award the business to another company.

When we realized why we had lost the bid to renew the OCCC contract, we did some fast research and found out that we could protest the bid outcome. It wasn't an easy process, but we figured it out and the initial bid decision was overturned in our favor. I've been told that in the entire history of the Orange County Convention Center, this was the only time a bid decision was successfully overturned. And it was because I don't take no for an answer.

Pay Attention to Politicians

When you're running a business, especially if you're operating nationally or even internationally, you must pay attention to what politicians are doing because it can have a huge impact on your company. I'm not talking only about the big issues like the Affordable Care Act (Obamacare), I'm talking about legislation that doesn't make the headlines but that could affect how you operate or even changes in the tax code that could affect how much you pay in taxes. Yes, I know it's easy to get disgusted with political shenanigans and you might prefer to just turn it all off, but you really need to pay attention. I can't count the number of times that being a news junkie has paid off for us because we were able to be proactive. About the only thing I watch on television is news and I also get news alerts from various online sources. I also read the industry trade publications to see what's going on that could affect us. We get newsletters on finance, tax, and accounting issues from our auditors.

It's a process of constant education, especially if you're in an expansion mode. For example, there are rules we have to follow in Detroit that are different than the rules we have to follow in Las Vegas. And the rules in any given area could change, which means just because you're in compliance today doesn't mean you'll still be in compliance next year when you're doing the exact same thing.

Another reason to pay attention to politicians is if you're going after government contracts or doing other work that might be in the public eye. That was another on-the-job lesson for me. If you want to operate in public or government space, you need the support of the politicians because they have the power and authority over decisions that affect you.

Remember, the politicians know politics and you know business. The politicians want to gain power and get reelected while you want to grow your company and make a profit. The respective knowledge base and goals of politicians and entrepreneurs are rarely in sync, but you must respect the power lawmakers have to help or hurt you. The degree to which you choose to get involved in politics is, of course, your personal choice. But don't take your eyes off the politicians.

Joining the Private Jet Club

I am definitely a frequent flyer. My business takes me all over the world and I enjoy leisure travel as well. Chuck Whittall, a good friend of mine who is a real estate developer and entrepreneur, had been telling me for years that I needed to buy a plane and I kept saying I couldn't afford it. One day we were out to lunch (which I had paid for) and he took the back of the receipt and wrote out all the math showing the economic advantages of having a plane.

I still didn't think I could afford it, but I took that receipt to my accountant to get his opinion. About six or eight weeks later, he said, "Okay, it's time, you can buy the plane." I wasn't sure he was serious, but then he added, "Either you're going to write a big check to the IRS or you can buy a plane."

Well, okay. Let's buy a plane!

Actually, we bought a jet. Having a jet may seem like a huge executive indulgence, but it's a genuine productivity tool because I'm able to travel on my schedule. And when we're not using the jet for company purposes, it's available for charter, so it produces some revenue. But make no mistake: owning a jet aircraft is a significant expense. I don't need to tell you what a nightmare commercial air travel is— congested terminals, long security lines, delays and cancelations, lost baggage, inconvenient schedules, and more. Even so, you can't compare the cost of a first class ticket to anywhere with the cost of owning a plane. The only justification for it is how much you value your time.

Many people use their company airplanes to schmooze their customers; there's nothing wrong with that. I use our company jet because I want to know that I can get home to be with my wife and kids on *my* schedule. If you want that kind of control of your life, you're not going to get it traveling at the mercy of an airline.

We bought our first plane in 2009 when the economy was in a major downturn. Yes, we saved a lot of money on taxes by doing it, but the real win for the plane was that we could sell more and do it more efficiently. We could go anywhere and be there when the customer wanted us to be. We could fly into smaller airports that were often closer to our customers than the large ones. So the plane gave us a competitive advantage at a time when everybody was scrambling for business.

If you look at economic cycles over the years, you'll see that a lot of big corporations get rid of their planes as part of cutbacks during hard times. But if you use the plane as a tool to best utilize your time and increase sales, the value is there.

Is the jet a status symbol? Sure. It's a true luxury, and whether or not it should, it impresses people. Is it reasonable for every entrepreneur to own a plane? Of course not. You need a profitable company of a substantial size and you need to do enough travel to make it worthwhile. But it's a great example of setting your priorities and then finding the right tools to follow through and get things done.

Accept the Evolution

I have loved my industry since LMG's beginning—and even further back, when I was in high school and formed the video club. But it's been a long time since I operated equipment at an event. Today I spend my time doing things I could never have imagined even 20 years ago. And in that process, the team below me is getting pushed up and being developed to take over as the organization continues to grow and expand. It's critical to identify your company's future leaders and invest in them. If you're an entrepreneur and you build a successful company, this transition is a natural evolution.

As we grew, the functions of my role as the company's owner and founder changed. I had to shed a number of responsibilities as I took on new and different ones required by a growing company. If I hadn't, our growth would have been restricted by the practical limitations of how much one person can do. The strategy that best supported our goals was for me to let go of things other people were capable of doing and spend my time doing the things that only I could do. So I did my job and got out of the way so the great people in our company could do theirs.

QTL: Quality Time Left

I was at a conference recently when I heard Jimmy Johnson, former coach of the Miami Dolphins and Dallas Cowboys, say, "QTL." We were talking about why he didn't want to coach another team. He recognized that throughout his life he'd made a lot of sacrifices for his career, missing his sons' events and that sort of thing, and now he's focused on quality time left. That resonated with me.

One of the things everyone has to face is the reality of time. We only have so much time and we don't know if it's a little or a lot. So we have to use what time we have wisely. Respect time, don't throw it away. Use it effectively. When you let yourself be distracted by things that are superficial or unimportant, when you procrastinate, when you ignore things that you should be doing, that's when time becomes the enemy.

> *Use your time wisely. Respect it, don't throw it away. Use it effectively.*

Something seems to happen magically to people, sometime around the 50 year mark: They figure out that they're not going to live forever. They might have known it when they were younger, but they didn't act like it, they acted like they were on a timeline to infinity. Then they wake up one morning and realize that their life is half over and they start looking at what they've accomplished—not just in business, but personally, in their families, with friends, in the community. When you're making choices in your life, both business and personal, make choices that will allow you to feel good about what you've done with the time you had. You can't change the past, but you can—starting right now—commit to practicing the philosophy of quality time left.

Chapter Four

Don't Be Afraid

When I was a teenager just getting started in this business, I felt no fear about anything I did. In large part that was because I didn't really understand the consequences of making a mistake. I was too inexperienced to grasp the scope of the work we were doing; I was having fun just doing what needed to be done. Today, I understand the scope of the work and consequences of failures, but I don't fear the outcome of any situation, and you shouldn't, either. You just do the best you can every day and ultimately what's going to happen is going to happen. And you just deal with whatever the circumstances are. Feeling fear is a waste of time and energy.

Learning to manage fear is important to business success. Some fears are reasonable and healthy—fearing a venomous snake or a wild animal on the loose can save your life. But that's not the sort of fear I'm talking about. The fears you need to master are the ones that pop up and stop you from doing what needs to be done, whatever that happens to be.

When I was a teenager still doing freelance work, I went to Nashville as a gofer on a car race. When the production crew needed some zip ties, I was sent to find them. They happened to be stored in an office where a meeting with the director and other top guys was in progress. I didn't have any idea how long the meeting was going to last and we needed those zip ties to get the equipment set up, so I quietly walked into the office, found what I needed, and was heading to the door when Fred Rheinstein said, "You know what I like about you, Les? You're relentless, you'll stop at nothing to get what you need done. Don't worry, we won't get in your way. You just get what you need." I don't think any of the people in that meeting were accustomed to a young gofer unapologetically entering their space, but Fred appreciated people who got their jobs done. Certainly that meeting was important, but so was what everyone else was doing. I was respectful, but I wasn't afraid to do my job.

The three fears you'll deal with in business most of the time are:

- Fear of rejection
- Fear of humiliation
- Fear of failure

Here's how you can deal with those fears: Learn to make them work *for* you instead of against you.

Fear of rejection and fear of humiliation often go hand-in-hand. They may cause you to not make a call, not ask a question, or not try to close a deal. But is rejection really so bad? Has anyone ever actually died from embarrassment? If you get rejected, at least you know where you stand and can decide what to do next. It's better to be rejected than to be left hanging because you didn't ask.

This may sound harsh, but in my opinion, people who don't take action because they fear rejection or humiliation are simply not very smart. When you go fishing, you never know what you're going to catch. But if you don't go fishing, you can be certain you won't catch any fish. If you want to catch fish, you have to bait your hook and get it in the water.

Don't fear rejection; see it as an opportunity. Go ahead and get the "no" so you can decide what to do next. And remember that this is business, so don't take it personally.

> *It's better to get a "no" than to not get an answer. At least with a firm rejection, you know where you stand.*

While I really don't understand how the fear of rejection or humiliation can make someone not do what needs to be done, I do understand the fear of failure. But it's not something I experience often and I don't let it stop me from trying—and you shouldn't, either. If you're going to do great things, you're going to have to take risks. And risk equals potential failure. Of course, you should do everything possible to mitigate that risk but if you haven't failed, you haven't taken enough risks. Instead of fearing failure, take action and, if it doesn't work, give yourself credit for trying.

Failure is Part of Success

Now that we've dealt with the *fear* of failure, let's talk about *actual* failure. From the business perspective, failure is when you try to achieve something and your plan doesn't work. The plan might not work because it's flawed, because of human error, because of a mechanical failure, or because of some external reason that's beyond your control. Sometimes the only person your failure will impact is you; sometimes it could be a small group of others; and sometimes it could be a substantial group that includes your customers and maybe even their customers. And that impact could be minor or major or somewhere in between.

Experiencing failure is an essential component of success. As entrepreneurs, we're taking a proverbial rubber band and stretching it farther and farther, trying to accomplish something we've never done before. Sometimes that rubber band is going to hold, sometimes it's going to break. In either case, we have conquered new ground because we've learned what works and what doesn't work. One of Thomas Edison's most famous quotes is, "I have not failed, not once. I've discovered 10,000 ways that don't work."

While Edison's attitude toward failure is one we should all develop, there's a psychological component to failure that we need to understand. It's natural for people to internalize their business failures, to make them personal, and to give them far more weight than they give successes. I'm a classic example: I *can't* tell you the top five successes we've had, but I *can* tell you the top failures—and I can do it in great detail. When we experience failure, it can take me weeks to recover emotionally. If you're like me, my advice is to take a lesson from professional athletes. When they lose a game, whether it was because of a mistake they made, a mistake someone else on their team made, or the opposing team just played better, they wake up the next day and play another game.

Something else I've learned about failure is that the more successful you are, the harder it often is to cope with failure. When you're used to doing it right, to being right, to winning, failure can be a painful punch in the gut that's going to hurt for a long time. Just keep reminding yourself that if you never experience failure, you're not risking enough. The key is to learn from your failures and use that knowledge to drive growth in your business.

> *When you're used to doing it right, to being right, to winning, failure can be a painful punch in the gut that's going to hurt for a long time.*

When it comes to failure, I see it this way: You can only fail at something over which you have absolute control. If you don't have absolute control and something goes wrong, *you* did not fail. In fact, under those circumstances, you often have a tremendous opportunity to succeed by being ready to deal with the situation.

In our business, there are so many potential points of failure. The light bulb in a projector can blow. A cable can break. The battery in a wireless microphone can go dead. Or the power in the facility can go out. We have a responsibility to deal with the situation by having backup equipment and plans in place. If the bulb blows or the cable breaks and we were prepared, we didn't fail. It would be a failure if we knew it was a possibility and we weren't prepared to handle it. It would be failure if we knew the right way to do it and we chose not to for some reason. And that describes a fear that I respect but that you rarely hear discussed: the fear of poor performance. If you promise Waldorf Astoria service and you deliver Motel 6, especially when you know better and the customer is paying for top service, that's a humiliating failure.

Just like rejection, when it comes to failure in business, don't take it personally. When you do the best you can and have prepared for every reasonable contingency, you just have to wait and see the outcome. Remember, the only way to avoid failure is to do nothing, which is a form of failure in itself. If the circumstances were within your control and you just screwed up, then yes, you failed. It's going to happen occasionally and it won't feel good. But you recover, you learn from the experience, and you keep going. Don't waste a lot of time beating yourself up over it; instead, take advantage of the opportunity to find a way to do it better the next time.

The Fallacy of Winning through Intimidation

Something I learned at a young age is that there's a right way and a wrong way to compete. I like winning as much as anyone, but in business, I believe in winning on the merits. There's also a right way and a wrong way to show respect to your customers. We treat our customers with courtesy and professionalism, and we are always honest and direct.

LMG was only about two years old when a big audiovisual services company expanded into Central Florida. During an event we were both working—LMG was providing a photographer and the other company was renting a projector—our photographer found out that the other company was over-charging for the projector. He went to the customer and persuaded him to rent the projector from us at our regular rate, which was substantially lower. Right after that, I got a call from the guy who was running that company's local office. I remember his exact words: "We're going to rub you out."

Obviously he'd been watching too many bad gangster movies. Maybe he thought that I would be easy to scare because I was so young. But at that age—I was either 18 or 19—I had no fear. I just kept doing what I was doing, serving my customers, growing my company. I didn't do any gigs with that company. Eventually they were bought out.

Our customers know they can count on us to keep their best interest in mind. If they ask for a particular piece of equipment and we think something else will serve them better, we advise them. If they're trying to do something at their event that just won't work, we explain why and offer alternative solutions. We don't stroke egos by telling them something is great when it isn't. We're not afraid to do the right thing for our customers, even when the right thing may cause us to lose money.

In business, people will watch you to try to determine if they have to worry about you, if they should fear you, or if you deserve their respect. You just need to show them what you're made of. When I was young and LMG was small, there were people who didn't take us seriously—and for many of them, that was a mistake. The competitors who didn't take us seriously lost business to us. The customers who didn't take us seriously missed out on our superior service and may have ended up with a lower quality supplier.

Over the years, we've earned the respect of our industry based on our performance. Our competitors have watched us grow and become a force to be reckoned with. Our customers have grown with us and allowed us to provide them with more and more services. And that's primarily because I'm not intimidated by competition and I'm not afraid to do what needs to be done to serve our customers and make our company successful. We've built a no fear culture and it has helped us accomplish some amazing things. When a company has resources (for us, those resources include a multimillion-dollar equipment inventory and some of the industry's top talent) and no fear, it becomes a formidable competitor. And

LMG is a formidable competitor.

Lawsuits are Lose-Lose

Life is short, paying lawyers is not fun, and time spent dealing with lawsuits is time you aren't spending growing your business. Even though we live in a litigious society, I'm proud that in more than 30 years, LMG has been involved in only one major lawsuit. And that lawsuit confirmed that my approach to conflict resolution is far preferable to litigation. It also taught me some valuable, albeit expensive, lessons.

Here's the story: We were 23 years old, profitable, and growing. We were a solid player in the industry, but still relatively small. And we had some great employees. Suddenly, over the span of maybe three weeks, several of our key employees resigned, all to go to work for a competitor company.

There are no words to describe the pain and anger I felt. I could deal with losing the people but I had to protect my company. So there I was, a guy who had never sued anyone in his life, in an attorney's office preparing to go to court for my company's survival.

I was possessed. I fought like there was no tomorrow. After three years, hundreds of thousands of dollars in legal fees, and untold hours of angst, we finally reached a settlement. And we did it without the attorneys. The owners of the two companies finally came together and found a solution we could all live with. I can tell you that we are absolutely a stronger, better company today because of this experience.

One of the most important things I learned during this process is that civil lawsuits are not about who is right or wrong, they're about who has the resources to fight. It's more than just the substantial legal fees, it's also the time and energy you and your senior people have to invest in the process. Many lawsuits are ultimately settled when the one or more of the parties either can't or don't want to fight anymore, either because they're out of money or they want to spend their time more productively.

The lawsuit also prompted us to make some significant changes in our internal procedures. We realized that our employment agreements were too vague and possibly not enforceable. We rewrote those documents to make them clear, specific and unambiguous, and took additional steps to protect our intellectual property.

Another positive outcome of the lawsuit is that all of our company agreements now include mandatory mediation and arbitration clauses. Whether the issue is with an employee, a customer, or a supplier, if we get to the point that we don't agree on something and we can't work it out between us, we're going to a mediator. If we can't settle the dispute at mediation, we will go to arbitration. Both sides to the dispute will get to tell their side of the story in the arbitration proceedings, the arbitrator will make a final decision, and we're done. No court, no jury, no lawsuits.

The money and time you spend on lawsuits is money and

time you aren't spending on building your company. I know there are some people who thrive on the drama, but I'm not one of them. For me, living in a lawsuit was like living under global thermonuclear war. We had to do it to save the company but I never want to go through anything like that again, and I don't recommend it for anyone else.

> *Money and time spent on lawsuits is money and time not spent on your business. Choose those battles carefully and wisely.*

Another good reason for avoiding lawsuits is that customers generally don't want to deal with suppliers who are quick to sue or are frequently sued. They don't want to risk getting sucked into a situation that is not of their making but that could cost them in legal fees and lost productivity just because they're doing business with you. Even though it might not have an impact on how you perform and regardless of whether you're a plaintiff or defendant, or you're right or wrong, you could lose business simply because you're a party to a lawsuit.

When it comes to litigation, your first goal should be to avoid it. The way we do that is to operate by a simple philosophy: We pay people what we owe them and we always try to do the right thing, no matter what the cost. If we have a misunderstanding or a conflict, we work hard to talk it through and find a win/win resolution. When we're at fault,

I'm not afraid to say, "I'm sorry. What do I have to do to make it right?"

When we are the victim, when we've suffered a loss because of the actions of another, I take an objective look at the situation and decide exactly how far I'm willing to go for restitution. I balance the principle of the situation against the cost of time and legal fees. Sometimes, even though I know we're in the right, I walk away because the fight just isn't worth it. Sometimes the principle is more important than the cost. And sometimes a calm analysis of the circumstances can lead us to a solution that doesn't involve litigation.

I know I'll always come out the winner by doing what's right and ultimately best for the company. Litigation should be your absolute last resort and only when it's over something that you're willing to go to the mat for.

If You Want the Answer, Ask the Question

I'm very inquisitive. I ask a lot of questions and I like people who ask a lot of questions. When I don't know something, I ask. I believe that being ignorant is not bad; staying ignorant is. To be ignorant is to lack knowledge. We are all ignorant about some things. But ignorance and stupidity are two different things. When I don't know something, I'm the first to admit it, and then I get the information I need. It's when you don't know something and aren't willing to make the effort to learn it that ignorance turns into stupidity.

Don't be afraid to ask anyone anything—remember, the

worst that can happen is that they won't answer you. The best thing is that you'll learn some valuable information.

When I got the idea to buy the projector that started LMG, I thought there was a need for large screen video projectors in Central Florida. But my dad suggested that I call some people and find out for sure. As I shared in Chapter 2, I didn't have a slick presentation. I just called some people I knew, told them what I was doing, and asked if they thought they might rent my projector—one simple question. Even today, I end every customer contact by asking, "What's your next project? What can we do to help you with it?" I know they need what we have to offer, I just need to find out more specifics so I can do what it takes to win the next gig.

Years ago, I met Robert Earl, founder of Planet Hollywood and other hospitality-related businesses, on a red-eye flight from Los Angeles to Orlando. I thought he was an incredible businessperson who had accomplished some amazing things, and I had the great luck to be sitting next to him in first class. So I started talking to him.

At the time, LMG was doing about $3 million a year, which is respectable but nothing compared to the business empire Earl had built. I asked him questions about how he ran a global business, how he maintained control, how he made his expansion decisions, and even how he managed his memorabilia collection. It was a long flight and we had time to talk about a lot of things, and he was more than willing to share his knowledge and experience with me. A few years later, I ran into him at a gas station (he doesn't live far from me) and I spoke to him. I couldn't imagine that he actually remembered me, but he seemed to. And I used to see him occasionally at Magic (Orlando's NBA team) games and he was always warm and friendly. Once he asked me how I was doing and I mentioned that I was thinking about taking my company public. He'd already gone through some spectacular successes and failures, and he cautioned me about some of the challenges involved in taking a company public. If I had been intimidated by who he was and afraid to talk to him on the plane when we first met, I wouldn't have had the benefit of a valuable connection and some excellent guidance.

When I would be at the Canon Business Solutions Club (a members-only club that was in the old Orlando Arena), I had the opportunity to meet and interact with a variety of movers and shakers like Earl and timeshare mogul David Siegel. I used to see Richard DeVos, the Magic's owner and the co-founder of Amway, at games. Once I was able to ask him, "What's life like owning a kick-ass basketball team?" (It happened to be a year that the team was playing especially well.) He said, "We're very blessed to have this basketball team, and we're going to keep it in the family." That might be what he says to everybody—I don't know, but I do know he was gracious to me.

My point in sharing these stories is this: I have always been completely comfortable talking to anyone at any level. I like to interact with people. I do it in a way that's respectful and courteous, not offensive, and they usually respond the same way. And that's how relationships begin.

If you don't open your mouth, you can't find out who you're with and what they do. And you'll never know if there was a potential relationship you could have pursued. If you don't feel comfortable asking questions, my advice is: Get over it. And if you don't feel comfortable asking for the business, you need to either figure out how to get past that and do it anyway, or you need to forget about being an entrepreneur.

Learn the Language of Business

The language of business is accounting and finance, and your success depends on an understanding of those issues. Many people who have great ideas find the numbers side of the operation a mystery and they're intimidated by even the most basic accounting terms like income, expenses, margin, and profit. If you don't have a solid understanding of accounting, you need to educate yourself, take classes, or have someone mentor you. If you don't, you risk making a lot of expensive mistakes.

I didn't start with a degree in finance—I started LMG and college at the same time. Especially in those early days, it was much easier for me to do the event than it was to learn how to run a business. But I learned. I began taking basic business courses in my freshman year and I'm sure I drove my teachers and probably my fellow students crazy with all the questions I asked. I was already operating my business in the real world; I would leave class and immediately apply what I learned.

Today when I'm invited to be a guest lecturer for business classes, one of the questions I often ask students is: How do businesses survive?

The responses are usually all over the place—on profits, by having a good product, a good marketing plan, being able to get and keep customers. While those things are important, the correct answer is far simpler.

Businesses survive on cash.

You either have it (or at least access to it) or you don't.

Cash to a business is like oxygen to a human—it is absolutely essential for survival. It's your lifeline. Without cash, you're like a car without fuel. You can't go anywhere.

The easiest way to find out if you have cash is to take a look at your bank account balance. If you have money in the bank, that's a good start. Then look at your available credit. If you have immediate access to a line of credit, that's as good as cash. And that's the most primitive level of understanding business finance.

Of course, if you're going to grow a successful business to any significant size, there's far more to finance than that. It's not enough to turn a profit, you need to do the right analysis to understand why you were profitable so you can keep doing it. And if you're not profitable, you need to be able to figure out where your problems are so you can correct them.

Studying financial statements is not the most exciting part of building a business for most entrepreneurs, but it's essential. You need to understand the basics of taxes and accounting. You can hire an accountant or a comptroller to do the actual work of keeping up with changes in tax law and pulling together the numbers, but you need to know what the numbers mean. And you need to review them regularly. If you don't, you won't be able to make sound decisions.

I take a look at our financial statements monthly. I compare how much business is being booked against our budget. I review the expenses to make sure we're not spending more than we should be. If we're not on track with booking business or if our costs are out of line, we evaluate what's going on and decide on a course correction. The idea is to watch the numbers and take prompt action based on what they're saying.

A friend of mine who is also a successful businessperson takes a different approach. He says he can look at the numbers on a quarterly basis and be fine. I disagree. If you're starting to go off course in January and you don't look at the numbers until April, you could be in big trouble before you realize it. But if you look at January's numbers in February and you see a problem, you can correct it before it causes a lot of damage. The same thing applies when you're doing things right—when you see positive trends, you want to understand them and reinforce them.

Beyond reviewing our numbers monthly, LMG goes through a full audit every year. This isn't required, but I believe it's smart. Bringing in an outside independent auditor is a way to test our processes and controls. It also tells our bankers and other creditors that the numbers we're producing on our financial statements are accurate and reliable. That means they're willing to give us extremely competitive interest rates because their risk is lower. And when we can keep our costs down, we can reflect those savings in our pricing.

Most successful entrepreneurs are like me: They choose a business because it's something they love doing. Once you understand impact of the numbers on your company, some of the passion you have for the mission of your company will transfer to the financial side and you'll see the results in growth and profitability. When you're comfortable with the numbers, you'll be able to make decisions without being afraid.

Chapter Five

It Takes Great People to Build a Great Company

I'm a pretty smart guy, but I don't know everything and I certainly can't do everything. So I surround myself with smart, talented people who know what I don't, can do what I can't, and are committed to our company and its mission.

When it's time to hire, you want to find people who love what they do, who see their work as a career not just a job, who will be committed to your company and passionate about the outcomes they produce. Putting these people on your team will super-charge your business and leave your competitors in the dust.

You need great people to make the machine run. Don't hire people who are just like you—you don't need a company full of entrepreneurs, you need a balance of leaders and followers, of managers and workers, of creative people and number-crunchers. Especially for your management or executive team, you want people who are complementary to you—your weaknesses need to be their strengths. Surround yourself with people who are smarter than you, who know things you don't, who have different skills and talents, who will complement you. And don't hire "yes men"—that might feed your ego, but it won't get you anywhere. You need people who will tell you the truth even if it means disagreeing with you.

Be very cautious when it comes to hiring friends. Especially when you're small and when you as the owner are doing a constant juggling act, it's easy to turn to your own social circle when you need to hire, but it's dangerous for your company, especially if your hiring decisions are based on a combination of you needing workers and your friends needing jobs with only minor consideration to their qualifications. It's essential that you be able to be objective about every employee's performance and that there is no actual or perceived bias or favoritism because of a personal relationship between you and any of your employees.

My policy has always been to keep my relationships with our employees separate from my relationships with my friends. We work in a casual environment and we are friendly, but there's a line we don't cross because I don't want to ever put myself in a place where I can't be objective and do what's best for the company. I also don't want to ruin a friendship over a work-related issue. Another reason to avoid hiring friends is that if and when the time comes that they decide to leave, they can make the decision based on what is best for them without worrying about the impact on your friendship.

There will come a time when you have to get out of first gear when it comes to hiring. The general rule should be: Find the best person you can afford to do the job that you need done, and stay away from friends so you can be totally objective about your employees' performance.

Taking Care of People is Taking Care of Business

I want everyone who works for LMG, whether as an employee or a freelancer, to care as much about our customers and the company as I do. The only way that can happen is if they know the company cares about them. That's much easier to accomplish when you're small and everyone knows everyone else and everyone also knows pretty much everything the company is doing. It gets more challenging as you grow.

There was a time that I knew every LMG employee—I didn't just know their names, I knew *them*. I knew about their personal lives, their families, and they knew me. We had a history. Now I probably only know about half of the people who work for LMG. Even though I wanted to grow the company, I admit that I miss the intimacy of the smaller group—it was a little happy family. Now we're a big family; we're still happy but now we have lots of branches and "distant relatives" in various locations.

Something that didn't occur to me in the early days and probably doesn't occur to most entrepreneurs when they're starting companies is that life is going to happen to your employees. They don't work in a vacuum. Employees are going to get married, get divorced, have babies, experience health issues and personal problems—and even die. And what happens in their lives is going to have an impact on other employees, the company, and sometimes even customers and suppliers. You should be prepared to deal with this, to give the necessary and appropriate support to employees and make sure the customers are taken care of. While I was working on this book, one of our technicians lost his wife; she was 51 years old when she died. His loss was tough for all of us, and I think he took some comfort in knowing that we were genuinely grieving with him.

There are plenty of resources for how to cultivate a loyal, productive team with compensation and benefit packages and so on, and we do many of those things. We find that investing in excellent benefits and a great working environment for employees generates a big return for the company. We recognize people for their performance and efforts. You can't give people unlimited raises forever. We've found that using other forms of recognition has value and employees consider it a tangible benefit. Not only do we recognize performance as a company, I personally go out of my way to express my appreciation to individuals for something they've done. I'm careful not to overdo it—everyone might get a paycheck, but not everyone gets a trophy. They have to earn the recognition by doing something special. Because they know that, the recognition has meaning to them. What it comes down to is this: When you have loyal, happy employees, you have a better chance to have loyal, happy customers.

Along with doing things that make your company a desirable place to work, you need to put sound employment policies in place. This is one of those chores like learning to read financial statements when you don't really care about numbers—it may not be the most exciting thing you do, but it's important. You need a system for recruiting, screening, and hiring that will help you identify the best candidates and protect you from charges of unfair employment practices. Procedures for everything from how to call in sick to how to do a particular job need to be clearly defined, as do the consequences for violating company policies.

Every employee should sign an employment agreement that clearly spells out the terms of your offer, incorporates company policies either directly or by referencing other documents, and includes appropriate confidentiality and non-compete language that protects your intellectual property. Have an experienced employment law attorney review all of your human resources-related documents and policies to make sure they comply with all applicable regulations, are non-discriminatory, and provide as much protection to your company as possible.

When Tough Times Mean Tough Decisions

I'm very proud of the fact that there's only been one time in LMG's history that we had to make a significant staff reduction through layoffs. It was after the terrorist attacks of September 11, 2001. People suddenly stopped holding meetings and events. Nonessential business travel was canceled. Overnight we went from a company that had enjoyed steady growth from day one to a company struggling with tough times and being forced to make sacrifices in order to survive. It may not sound like a big deal to say we reduced our staff by about 12 percent, but we never lost sight of the fact that every employee we let go was a person with a family. We were as compassionate as we could be, but we did what had to be done for the survival of the company.

When you're facing challenges due to circumstances beyond your control, you have to make decisions that are best for the company. And if those decision include reducing your workforce, you should do it in a way that is best for the employees who will remain and be serving your customers.

It's usually easy to identify the great performers because they are the leaders, they're the ones that consistently demonstrate initiative, they're clearly committed to the company and their careers. Those are the people you want to keep. It's also fairly easy to identify the marginal performers, the ones who just do their jobs and never go the extra mile. When you have to cut staff, that's where you start. You may like these employees as individuals, but you can't keep them when the survival of your company is at stake.

Pull the Weeds

Note that I didn't suggest that you begin a layoff such as we had to do in 2001 by terminating the poor performers. You shouldn't have those people on your team in the first place. Regardless of what's going on in your organization—whether you're growing and making money hand over fist or you're struggling to survive—you have a responsibility to continually weed out the people who don't belong.

When people are not the right fit for the job or the company and you let them go, you're doing the best thing for them as well as the company. You're giving them the opportunity to find something they'll enjoy and be happier with—and maybe even really love. It's not easy to let people go, but you have to recognize that sometimes you're going to have people who may have seemed right when you hired them but who turn out to be wrong for the job or your company. Getting fired isn't always a bad thing. It can open doors for people to go places they might not have considered before. Remember, Steve Jobs was very publicly fired from Apple, the company he co-founded, and went on to co-found NeXT and launch Pixar Animation Studios. Getting fired from his job at Standard Oil gave Robert Redford the motivation to pursue his acting dreams. And right before they started Home Depot, Bernie Marcus and Arthur Blank were fired from their jobs at Handy Dan, a home improvement chain that went out of business in 1989.

Sometimes getting fired is a kick in the butt for people who have gotten comfortable. When people get to the point that they think so highly of themselves that they believe they have nothing left to learn, it's time for them to move on.

In any business environment, comfort equals stagnation. Innovation never happens with stagnation. People don't discover new things or figure out how to do things better when they aren't challenged. If you don't keep making yourself better, you get rusty. There's no standing still. If you're not moving forward, you're moving backward. Remember, one of our core values is continuous improvement. Those values aren't just feel-good words posted on the wall—we live them every day in everything we do.

The people who don't share my vision generally don't stick around. They're not comfortable in our environment. And if they don't leave on their own, we encourage them to find opportunities elsewhere.

> *When people get comfortable, they often stagnate—and stagnation blocks innovation and growth.*

People who are more interested in blocking and stopping than they are in achieving become obstacles themselves. They're like weights that just drag you down. Relieve yourself and your organization of those people and let them go find opportunities that they're going to genuinely love.

There are three kinds of people I won't keep on my team—and you shouldn't keep on yours:

1. People who think that average is good enough. I'll talk more about that in Chapter 6.

2. People who focus on why things can't be done rather than how they can be done.

3. People who tell me what they think I want to hear instead of what they really think.

Growing Pains

When I first started LMG, I wore just about every hat: sales, technician, transportation, administration, whatever else needed to be done. Though I was fascinated by the technology, I gravitated more toward sales and began hiring people to work the events while I developed business. When you start hiring people, you have to give them something to do and that means relinquishing some control—something that's not easy for most entrepreneurs, and it wasn't for me. But there were only 24 hours in a day and I knew my time was best spent bringing in the business and letting others work the gigs.

Until LMG hit about 25 people, everybody reported directly to me. As we grew, that became inefficient and ineffective. It wasn't possible for me to manage that many people and do everything else I needed to do. I realized we needed a management level, but adding it turned out to be a lot harder than I expected.

In a technical business like ours, it seems that the people doing the work only respect other people if they have equal technical skill and knowledge. In the early days of LMG, I knew how to operate every piece of equipment we had and I did most of the training. (Things have changed. I'm not allowed to touch the equipment anymore.) While the people I worked with *recognized* me as the owner of the company, they *respected* me in part because there wasn't an aspect of the operation that I wasn't familiar with. I've seen that dynamic over and over again, not only within LMG but at other companies. Technical people don't appreciate supervisors and managers for their strong managerial skills unless they also have technical knowledge.

The first thing I did to add managers was approach three key employees that had been with us for at least seven or eight years and who I thought had leadership potential. I took them out to lunch with our CFO and laid out the proposition. "We want you to be part of something bigger, something that's growing. Our company is expanding and we need people to run it," I said. "So instead of being an hourly employee working events as a technician, we want you to be a manager. You'll be paid a salary of $60,000 (remember, this was the late 1980s when that was a significantly higher than average salary) instead of the roughly $75,000 you're making as an hourly worker, but you'll be a leader, part of the management team, and as the company grows, your position and compensation will grow."

Not a single one of those employees was interested in my offer. Their focus was not on the potential of the new position, but on how much per hour they would make as a manager instead of doing the actual technician work. They didn't want to take what they saw as a pay cut. I said, "You don't understand. Yes, you'll make less money in salary now, but in the long run as we grow, you'll make more."

They still couldn't see it. I let them know the management level was going to be created no matter what they chose. I wanted to promote from within, but without any qualified people willing to accept the new jobs, I had to bring people in from outside—something that is often not well-received in organizations, and it certainly wasn't for us.

The technicians didn't like being managed. There were so many of them when they were all reporting directly to me that I wasn't supervising them closely. The jobs were getting done, the customers were happy, we were profitable, and the technicians were making money. But part of the process of effective management is to watch the labor hours and make scheduling decisions that are best for the company, and that's what the new management team did. And suddenly the technicians (all of them, not just the ones who had turned down the management offer) weren't making as much money because they weren't working as many hours.

Equally important was that they resented the new organizational structure. Some of them saw the fact that they no longer had immediate, direct access to me as a step backward. We even had a few people attempt to sabotage the new managers we brought in. Finally, things settled down, but it was a process, it took time, and it wasn't easy.

One of the interesting things about this process is that within a few years, those three people who I had identified as potential leaders and who had been with us at least seven years each were all gone. They moved on to other jobs. I think a big part of the reason was that they were used to dealing with me directly and when we added a layer of management, they resented it. Another interesting thing is that many of the people who were right behind them that were working through our ranks, people I thought showed potential but weren't quite ready for management at the time, are still with us and are some of our leaders today.

Then we reached the next level of growth and had to do it all again. An added element to the second time we reorganized was that some of the people who helped us get to that point simply weren't qualified to go further. We had to make some difficult and even painful decisions.

The reality is that someone who can help you take your company from $1 million to $10 million probably doesn't have the skills to help you go from $10 million to $25 million. This is not a negative reflection on them, it's an honest assessment of their capabilities. I'm very thankful for those people and their contributions, and I made sure they were well compensated. But I let them go when I realized it was the best thing for them and for LMG. It's important to understand that, as you grow, you will have people who won't be comfortable with how your environment is changing. That's not good or bad, it doesn't mean there's anything wrong with them, they just don't fit anymore and it's better for everyone if they move on to a place that's a better match.

I've had to go through this process three or four times to build a team with the technical and management ability to grow LMG past the $100 million level and handle its acquisition by Entertainment Technology Partners. What I've learned through the experience is that it's essential for you, the owner or CEO, to define what the next level is and then align yourself with people who share your vision and have the ability to help you reach it. You want people who are part of the team and committed to the outcome. Most important, they have to be people who don't stop when they hit a roadblock, but instead figure out how to get around it and keep going.

Your systems and processes are also going to suffer from growing pains. You have to be sure that the machine that was humming along putting out 100 widgets a day can put out 125, 150, or more as demand increases. Don't wait until the machine breaks down to figure out what you're going to do when you can meet demand. Monitor the machine so you know what to reinforce or change as well as what you need to do when the machine reaches its maximum capacity. This applies to systems as well as equipment. Many of the systems that worked for us when we were a $25 million or even a $50 million company simply don't work now that we've topped

$100 million. It doesn't matter what your business is, what systems you have, what processes you use—it's not going to work when you double your volume unless you've prepared in advance by making changes that allow you to scale what you do.

These are some of the problems created by success, and they're nice problems to have. In 2014, we grew 25 percent, which was double the growth we had projected and prepared for. We were fortunate to have that additional business, but along with that unexpected business came the unexpected work of making sure we could handle it. But because we'd been through this process of reorganizing to accommodate growth, we were able to meet the increased demand.

As we continue to grow, I'm always trying to figure out what's going to break next. I don't say that to be cynical; on the contrary, it's a very positive outlook because I know how much growth can strain your operations capacity. This is also an opportunity to make improvements. If you don't look for ways to improve operationally as you grow, the growth will choke you.

> *More business means more work. Be sure you're ready to handle the additional work your growth plans will generate.*

Depending on your particular industry, you may be able to design your systems and processes so they are scalable and can grow without a lot of modifications along the way. Just keep in mind that while the output of some machines may be scalable, you also have the human factor. What do you need in the way of human capital to run those machines?

When you're growing, it's easy to think that increasing the budget or hiring more people will solve a problem. That's rarely the case. Don't just throw money or bodies at a problem. Get to the root of the issue and come up with real solutions.

Though we are an excellent company with a reputation for superior performance, I don't believe anything we do would qualify as the absolute best way. There's always room for improvement. No matter how good you're doing, as you continue to grow, you'll have to figure out how to do it better.

Making Long-Term Commitments

Don't confuse the necessity of management evolution with the value of long-time employees. We have a lot of people who have been with LMG a long time, some all the way back to the early days before any of us realized the company's potential. These are talented people who love their craft and are always learning and sharpening their skills. They're committed to LMG and, in turn, we treat them well. I believe that if you want to work with the best people, you have to invest in those people to make sure they continue to be the best. We do that in a multitude of ways—coaching, seminars, courses, books, conferences, technical training, whatever it takes to give them the education they need to stay at the top of their game. We send Dave John, our chief operating officer, to Harvard where he takes classes in critical business thinking and gains knowledge that would be difficult to learn in any other venue. We have an outside training coach who comes in and mentors our management team. Everyone has the opportunity to continue their education so they can stay sharp and be on the leading edge of their profession. Training is a constant need in our business because we're working with ever-changing technologies and sophisticated equipment. People who come to work with us and don't take advantage of this usually don't stay long. But if you like learning, you'll love working at LMG.

As I explained in Chapter 2, one of our core values is continuous improvement. Someone who is satisfied with the status quo will find it very hard to work here. We could have the best of the best and we're still always thinking: What can we do to make it better? We don't coast on our successes. We use success to create momentum, to do more, to do it better.

> *Someone who is satisfied with the status quo will find it very hard to work here.*

It's essential that you trust the people on your team. You have to be comfortable trusting them with your resources, assets, money, decision-making, power, and customer relationships. You want them to use their intelligence and talent (after all, that's why you hired them), but you also want them to function in your business according to your philosophy. When my employees make decisions, I want them to do things based on WWLD – what would Les do? My philosophy is more about doing the right thing than it is about making a profit on the work. People need to know that you're committed to always doing the right thing. That's the only way they can completely trust you.

When you surround yourself with smart people and you create an environment where it's safe for them to be honest, they will help you move in the right direction. You need people who don't say, "That can't be done," but instead say, "The approach you're suggesting won't work for this reason. I suggest we try doing it a different way." You need people who will challenge you and that you can challenge. Those are the people we have on our team, and when they tell me things, I listen. I don't always agree, but I listen.

> *Surround yourself with smart people and create an environment where it's safe for them to be honest so they can help you move in the right direction.*

It's really quite simple: Doing the right thing creates good karma. Doing the wrong thing intentionally creates bad karma. And karma is a bitch.

Hire Happy People

I've always said that happiness is not a destination, it's a way to travel. It's much easier to build a successful company when you staff it with happy people. Happy people—people who like what they're doing and who they're doing it with—produce better results. Unhappy people can bring others down. So make it a practice to hire happy people.

Attitudes are contagious. That's why I made a conscious decision years ago to not work with grumpy or cynical people. Of course, I understand that everyone is going to have an occasional bad day. We all have challenges and losses that cause emotions such as sadness, grief, and even anger. What I'm talking about here is a general attitude and approach to life that's positive and upbeat. I don't like even being around unhappy people. If people want to be miserable, they're not going to do it on my watch.

Happiness is priceless. It's something inside of us that you can't quantify, you just know what it is when you feel it—and when you don't feel it. And when you're happy, other people can see it. When I meet someone, I can tell immediately whether they're happy or grumpy, even before they speak, because of the vibe they project.

How can we define happiness in terms of the workplace? I believe it's the feeling that what you're doing has purpose. It's being part of something that's bigger than yourself. It's being a member of a successful team. It's being treated with respect. It's performing well. It's having the right tools to do your job. It's being listened to when you have ideas. And in our business, it's the applause at the end of the show.

Happy people have potential because they look for the

good in life. They tend to be optimistic. For them, it's not about what we can't do, it's about how we're going to get it done. It doesn't matter how skilled or experienced someone is, if they're not a generally happy person, they're not a fit for LMG. But if they're upbeat and positive, if they have the basic ability and are willing to learn, they'll do well with us. For example, I met our current human resources manager when she was working as a receptionist at a gym I belonged to. She was always so happy that I wanted her to come work with me. Eventually she accepted my offer (I'm tenacious), she has grown with us, and she's a tremendous asset to our organization.

Your decision to staff your company with happy people starts with you—you need to be happy or you can't expect the people around you to be happy. That's why it's so important to choose a business where you can do something you love. It's important to understand what lifts you up and what brings you down. I've found that doing things to make someone else happy makes me happy, whether it's something as simple as bringing lunch to my assistant or as significant as supporting a charity.

When you have a company staffed with happy people, there is no limit to what you can accomplish.

Chapter Six

Average is Unacceptable

Whatever you do, don't be average. Be exceptional. Decide what you're going to do and work diligently toward being the absolute best at it.

Deep down in my core being, I believe that being average is unacceptable and working your hardest to be exceptional is a minimum standard. That's what I tell people whenever I get the chance, whether it's students when I'm teaching a class, our employees, or even my kids. If you want to build something great, you can't do it with average people.

From the time I was a young child, I have been driven by two simple things:

- Wanting to be the best, to be absolutely

exceptional at what we do.

- Not being satisfied with the status quo.

Note that I said these are simple things, but I'm well aware they are not necessarily easy. They require effort and hard work.

I push everyone who works with me to their limit to get the best out of them. Let me clarify that I'm not cracking a proverbial whip, I don't make threats, I just let them know what I expect and, perhaps more important, that I believe they can do it. My expectations are very high, but they're not unrealistic. And if people need a little help to produce outstanding results, we do our best to give them the assistance and support that will get them to the next level. But if average is the best they can do, they're the wrong person for the job.

> *If you want to build something great, you can't do it with average people.*

Some might think that's harsh and callous. I think it's just good business. I'm loyal to LMG's employees and freelancers and I expect loyalty in return. However, while I believe loyalty is a good thing, displaced loyalty can hurt you. Among other things, it can stunt your growth. When you keep people where they can't do their best, where they can't help you, it's not loyalty—and you're certainly not being kind to them or fair to yourself. You're not doing people a favor by letting them be less than their full potential.

When a company grows, it changes. As I explained in

Chapter 5, that evolution will likely identify people who have done a great job in the past but who are no longer a fit for your organization. You owe people who work with you the opportunity to grow, to do well, and to be successful, but they are not entitled to a job just because they've worked with you over a period of time. Certainly when you have to terminate a long-term employee, whether it's for cause or not, you should do it fairly and with kindness and compassion. When people are no longer serving your company or themselves, it's time for them to move on to a place where they can be effective.

Excellence is the Only Option

I've heard average defined as the "cream of the crap." I agree—it's the best of the worst. At LMG, excellence is the only option. That doesn't mean everything is always going to run smoothly. In fact, we know we can count on challenges. We're prepared and when things aren't going right, we work on a solution.

Another element of excellence is initiative. You want people who demonstrate initiative, who aren't afraid to speak up and take action. Someone who knows there's a problem and ignores it instead of trying to solve it is *not* the kind of person you want on your team.

Excellence means doing whatever it takes to make sure the customer's show is perfect—or at least looks perfect to the audience. In the early days, my customers knew they could call me in the middle of the night to tell me they needed a piece of gear on a show, and I would get out of bed, run to the shop, pack up what they needed, drive to the airport, and have it on the next flight out to wherever it needed to go. We still offer that level of response.

People in the live event business need to understand that their suppliers have their backs no matter what happens. That's what we do. We know that while our clients might be at least somewhat sympathetic to the challenges we're dealing with (such as equipment failures, transportation delays, and other situations beyond our control), the bottom line is that they want what we promised, and anything else is just an excuse. We don't make excuses.

I'm wired to play to win. I'm driven by a competitive spirit. I started out as a David in an industry full of Goliaths, and I've now become one of the Goliaths. I didn't do that by being average or by accepting an average performance from the people on my team.

You Can't Intimidate People into Excelling

It's not unusual for employees to be intimidated by the company's founder or senior management. I don't feel like I'm an intimidating person, but when it was brought to my attention that sometimes I appear that way, I began making a conscious effort to change that perception.

People who are intimidated will not perform at their highest level. Intimidation is *not* a good motivation tool. Certainly managers must maintain their authority but it doesn't need to be done through fear. Respect is woven through our core values because it creates an atmosphere where people can and will excel.

When people join our company, here's what I tell them: "If we have a problem with a customer at two o'clock in the morning and you have the knowledge or ability to solve that problem, I will call you and wake you up to get your help, and I will not apologize. I will take care of our clients no matter what. And it goes both ways. You have my number and you can call me at any time, night or day." My goal is to set an expectation so they understand that what we do is mission critical, it's time-sensitive, and we must perform. I have made and received plenty of middle-of-the-night calls and I hold everyone to that standard. Because I make it clear that the customer's needs come first, it helps remove the intimidation factor and lets people know they don't need to be afraid to do anything that is necessary to deliver the best results to our customers.

The Exceptional Perspective on Change

One thing exceptional people have in common is that, rather than resisting change, they find the opportunities in every situation. Here's an example: As I've said, relationships are the foundation of our business. Our relationships are not just with the companies, but with the individuals. I remember the first time a person I'd been working closely with at one customer moved to another company. I was concerned about the impact that change would have on us—would his replacement continue to use us or bring in another supplier?

I quickly learned that any time there's a regime change in an organization, it means double opportunity for suppliers. First, you have the opportunity to gain business at the new company with a person who already knows and trusts you. Second, you have the opportunity to build a relationship with the new decision-maker at your current customer. We've never bothered to figure out exactly how much of our business has come from people we've worked with who have either gone to work for different companies or who have started their own companies, but I know it's substantial.

Change doesn't always happen overnight, but it's inevitable. It's a matter of when, not if. For a business to grow, it must change; that applies to your customers as well as to you. How you deal with change both personally and as an organization, how you position yourself to work through the obstacle course that may come with change, will greatly impact your success.

Our company culture is one that sees voluntary and involuntary change as positive. We regularly make changes to improve our service. We're always asking ourselves if we are doing the absolute best we can and if there's anything we can do to get better. If there is, it's time for a change. When the change is driven by circumstances out of our control, our first response is: How do we turn this into a beneficial outcome for us and our customer?

You will have people in your organization who resist

change. That's human nature. It may be because they've gotten complacent, or their skills are limited, or they don't understand the new technology. Whatever the reason, you need to decide how much you want to invest in helping them accept the changes you feel are necessary. And as I've already said, if they can't accept those changes, they need to go.

Playing the Super Bowl Every Day

The bigger your business becomes, the bigger the stakes are for everything you do. More money is involved, more people are affected. It's like going from the regular season to the playoffs and ultimately to the Super Bowl. You won't get to your Super Bowl if you don't try to be the best at what you do and if you don't consistently play to win. And when you're in the Super Bowl and you win, you win big. But when you lose, you lose big as well.

As your company grows, there will likely be a point when you feel like you're playing the Super Bowl every day. It's when your jobs go from thousands to millions—and so do your mistakes. It's a big responsibility, but it's also exhilarating. It's why you started the business in the first place. And it's why average is simply unacceptable.

Make a Place for Top Talent

Whatever the size, exceptional companies are staffed by exceptional people, and exceptional people won't necessarily be looking for a job when you're ready to hire. Always be on the lookout for top talent and be flexible enough to make room for those people when you find them.

Years ago I met a kid who was working as an audiovisual technician at one of the big hotels in Phoenix. He had a great attitude (remember, I like happy people), which is why he caught my attention. I knew he would be an asset to LMG, so I offered him a job. We doubled his hourly rate (he deserved it; the company he'd been working for was seriously underpaying him) and provided an opportunity for him to hone his skills. He did a fantastic job while he worked with us, but he really didn't want to be a technician, he wanted to be a programmer. He ultimately left us to start his own company and created a software package that's very popular in our industry—in fact, we use it today.

A decade or so after he launched his product, I ran into him at an event. He thanked me for giving him the opportunity to get a better understanding of our industry and said I could take partial credit for his success. But what I saw was a bright young man with initiative and drive. I hired him and he did an excellent job for us. He also saw a need in the industry and figured out a way to meet it with the software package he created. I told him, "I'll take credit for identifying great talent, but you did all the work and you should be very proud of what you created."

If you stay on the lookout for top talent and bring exceptional people on board when you find them, you're likely to be the catalyst for your people doing all kinds of great things. Whether they do those things for your company or they have to go somewhere else to achieve their goals, you'll still benefit from the time they were with you and you can take satisfaction in knowing you had an impact on their lives.

Fun is Essential

While average is unacceptable, a sense of humor and the ability to have fun working in a high-stress environment are essential if you're going to deliver an exceptional product or service. We ask a lot of our people and it's important that they're able to enjoy what they do and relieve their stress by joking around. In fact, I'm a popular target of pranks by both our own team and by our customers—especially the ones who have been with us a long time. From the days of working for Big Les when I was in high school, I've seen the importance of humor and fun on the job. That's probably why I understand it now.

There are times, of course, when we have to get serious and focused because there's a critical deadline to meet or a major problem to solve. When that happens, it's like hitting the overdrive button. But it takes a lot of energy to be in that super-hyper mode all the time. People are much more productive when they're working in an atmosphere where they can relax and be themselves.

Serve More than Your Customers

Exceptional companies staffed by exceptional people serve more than the customers—they serve their community. LMG has always been a good corporate citizen and has responded to the needs of the community with cash and in-kind donations. As we approached our 30th anniversary, I felt like we needed to do more.

In the past, we had celebrated company anniversaries with a party. But you don't really touch anyone's life in a permanent way with a party. I felt like it was time to do something different, something more meaningful. We decided to make our anniversary celebration last a full year, from March 2014 through March 2015, during which time we'd identify and support 30 great causes, one for each year we'd been in business. We called it the "30-in-30" campaign. At that time, we had six locations across the country and every office participated. Participation was voluntary, but the response from the employees was amazing. Giving back never felt so good.

We set a few guidelines for the charities. I like to do things that directly help people within the geographic area of where we live and work, so the charities had to have a strong local presence. We went through a list of 50 or 60 charities and cut a lot of them because I either didn't understand their work or I didn't understand how contributing was going to help people. Once the 30 charities were identified, we turned our people loose. They collected and donated supplies for local food banks and animal shelters, they ran races and raised money through sponsorships, they donated blood, and they identified opportunities for the company to make donations while the employees served. For example, we donated gear to a fundraiser for Hope & Help, an agency whose mission is to save lives by treating and preventing the spread of HIV/AIDS in Central Florida. For another project, the company donated food and employees served a special meal at a shelter for domestic violence victims; in addition to their time, our employees made personal donations to the shelter.

The goal wasn't to make a big public splash, it was to make a difference. And we did. I believe that if you're doing well, you have a moral responsibility to find a cause to support and share your good fortune. Your choice of a cause could be driven by a personal experience or just be something that matters to you. The support can be through your company but shouldn't be as a promotion of your company. It's certainly acceptable to make donations in an effort to promote your company, but that's not charity, it's marketing.

Our goal with the "30-in-30" campaign was to support the communities that support us and we spent a substantial amount of money on it. But we got a degree of payback I wasn't anticipating in how our people responded. They loved the program and it made them feel good about themselves and the company. And those feelings manifested in stronger commitment and superior performance at every level.

Chapter Seven

Persuade, Negotiate, Close

At a young age, I realized that I love selling. I don't mean selling in its lowest, most superficial form of pressuring people to buy something they don't want, won't use, can't afford, and that's probably overpriced to begin with. I'm talking about the power of persuasion, of providing vision and leadership whether it's closing a mutually-beneficial business transaction with a customer or supplier, inspiring employees to perform at their best, or convincing investors to invest or bankers to lend.

A primary function of leadership is seeing the future and persuading people to help you get there. Whether instinctively or by training, great leaders often have strong selling skills. For me, being in a sales environment is like a shot of pure adrenaline. It doesn't matter how tired or distracted I am, I wake up, my eyes light up, and I'm energized. Talking about what we do and how we can make magic and pixie dust for our customers is one of the key things that makes me tick.

Not long ago, I made a presentation to a customer in a coffee shop in New York. When I was finished and the customer had left, a man sitting at the next table said, "You are so passionate about what you do." I was a little taken aback by the obvious eavesdropping, and I said, "Do I know you?" He said, "No. I'm an HR recruiter. Would you be looking for an executive? I have a perfect person for you." As it happens, his candidate wasn't "perfect" for us, but my point in sharing this story is that my passion for selling LMG's services is so great that strangers comment on it. That's how you should feel about your company.

Sometimes selling involves helping people realize a need they might not know they have. I learned that when I was in high school selling at flea markets. Most of the time people at the flea market would walk by not even looking at the tables. That didn't make sense to me because I assumed they were there looking for things to buy, but I quickly recognized the behavior pattern. So instead of just standing behind the table waiting for people to stop, Keith and I would be out in front, greeting people and saying things like, "You don't know you need this stuff, but come and get it." I think some people bought from us just for the entertainment we offered, but I didn't care. In fact, I've been told that even today my sales presentations are shows in themselves. If a high-energy, amusing presentation helps get us the business, that's all that matters.

Building the Right Sales Team

At LMG, we are the experts in what we do. When we're working with our customers to bid on a job, we're not content to just take an order for this many of these gadgets and that many of those widgets. We find out what their vision is and we put together a proposal that will help them reach and often exceed it. We educate them about new technologies that can enhance their events. We give them options they might not be aware of.

Most of our account executives have been with LMG for a long time. In our industry, it's not enough to have strong sales skills, you must also have a high degree of technical knowledge to understand our products and the customers' needs. And it helps to have a few ounces of craziness mixed in. Selling in our business is not a nine-to-five proposition. You have to feed on the crazy long hours, the dark production rooms, the ballrooms in venues all over the country (or world), the long rehearsal schedules—you have to thrive on this live experience that you're an essential part of.

Finding people with that ideal combination of knowledge, skill, and talent is not easy, and you don't get those top people by simply throwing dollars at them. Yes, there can be great monetary rewards in doing what we do, but often the real reward, the thing that truly motivates us, is sitting in the audience and hearing the applause. In most industries, the salespeople might not see where the product ultimately gets deployed or how people ultimately experience it. In our industry, our account executives are involved from the first conversation until the last light goes out on the production. They, along with our entire team of technicians and support staff, help develop, design, build, and execute. Then they tear it all down and do it again for another customer. It's a wonderful cycle that's always fresh, new, and exciting.

As a profession, sales is an entrepreneurial experience if you have some degree of ownership in the channel, whether you're paid on commission or you're actually purchasing a product and selling it to someone else. The sales superstars in every industry all have at least some entrepreneurialism in their DNA.

When you are a salesperson, you have to persuade others to join you on this journey that begins with closing the deal and doesn't end until long after the product or service is delivered and either placed into service or consumed. Fundamental, long-term success in sales can only come when you're selling something you believe in and that you're passionate about. I was fortunate to find that something at a young age and to not only sell it but to build a business on it. At the same time, I respect and appreciate that not everyone who enjoys and excels at sales wants to have their own business. If they did, we wouldn't have the topnotch sales team that we do.

Hard Work and Timing

The band Train has been a client of LMG Touring for years; how they came on board with us is a combination of perseverance and luck. When Craig Mitchell, the director of LMG Touring, took over the division, he started contacting every tour manager he could identify. He did online research to figure out who he needed to talk to for specific acts and what they had scheduled, and started making calls. Train was one of his target accounts; he finally found out who the tour manager was but couldn't find his contact information. He got a break when someone told him Train had switched management companies; when he called, he reached the band's manager who offered to put him in touch with the tour manager. It was perfect timing.

With the new management company, the previous manager's vendor relationships were off the table and they were looking for new resources. It was the ideal time to present LMG Touring.

We flew the manager to Orlando to see our facility and meet our people. He saw how committed we were and how much we wanted the account. At the end of his visit, he told Craig: "I will give you this account if, when I call, you always answer the phone and it never goes to voice mail." We've never had a customer make that specific request before. Craig promised and he's delivered; the manager's calls are always answered personally by Craig.

At the time, Train was in the process of making a

comeback. The first tour we did for them was relatively small. But now, the band is playing at the amphitheater level and it's a major account.

There are several important lessons in this story: You have to work hard to find the right contacts so you can make your pitch. You can't control the timing of what's happening with your customers—and sometimes you just get lucky and are in the right place at the right time. Always be ready for that to happen. Sometimes the issue that will close the deal is something that might never have occurred to you. And small accounts often grow into large accounts, so nurture them.

Closing the Deal

In LMG's early days, I was the sales department and pretty much everything else, too. I did it all—prospected for new accounts, put together the bids, made the presentations, closed 80-90 percent of the proposals, and worked most of the gigs. Today, of course, we have an outstanding team of sales professionals who are supported by equally outstanding customer service, technical, and operations professionals.

I never had any formal sales training. Some people just have sales in their DNA. In my opinion, sales training programs are like teaching someone to bake a cake. You can read the instructions and bake a cake. I can read the instructions and bake a cake. We'll both end up with a cake, but the cake you bake and the cake I bake will be different, maybe by a little or maybe by a lot, but different. That's because we both have knowledge and experiences that affect how we interpret the instructions.

Can you teach anyone a sales system? Yes. Anyone who wants to can learn techniques like qualifying the prospect to be sure they are the decision-maker and have the ability to pay, identifying needs, ways to ask questions, and so on. But you can't turn someone who doesn't have sales in their DNA into a great salesperson merely by teaching skills. If you've got sales in your DNA, then you need to hone that characteristic, keep it sharp and polished, and use it.

To be a good salesperson, you need to be able to build relationships and find out what it's going to take to get the business. Just listen to the customer. You need to pay attention to the words they're saying and understand what they're really asking. That's going to tell you what they want to buy, whether it's price, technology, or a solution to a problem they haven't figured out. You need to find their hot button—the thing that's going to get them to pull the trigger and say, "Yes, I'll buy that."

In our industry, most jobs require bidding. The customer puts out a request for proposal (RFP) with all the specs, and the suppliers respond according to the terms. Somewhere during the process, if we do a good job preparing our bid, we usually get to make a face-to-face presentation. That's where we shine. We understand it's not enough for the people on the other side of the table to know that we have the ability to do the job, they have to know that we're the best answer, that we're the right provider for them.

If you get an RFP and all you do is put numbers on the paper and turn it back in, you have very little chance of winning the bid—unless it's a commoditized bid, the customer is primarily interested in price, and you can be the low-cost provider. It's important to take the time to really understand the bid, to get sufficiently involved in the process that you can sell value. We don't like bidding without a meeting because it doesn't give us the opportunity to make that personal connection that's so important for many clients. But sometimes you have no choice because that's the way the customer operates, and that's when you have to craft a bid so compelling that you either win the job or at least win an opportunity to present in person. As I explained in Chapter 3 about what we learned with the Orange County Convention Center, it's essential that your bids be well-organized and thorough so the people evaluating them will have the information they need without questions.

Thanks in large part to the explosion of information available on the internet, more and more products and services are becoming commoditized. Customers are doing research online, gathering information that they used to get from sales representatives but doing it without any meaningful connection with the source. The way to combat commoditization of your product or service is by taking the initiative to establish and build relationships. You have to meet your prospects, in person if possible, but at the very least over the phone, and show them what differentiates you from everyone else. If you're going to persuade them that you're the right solution, they have to see something in you that's substantially better than anyone else.

Once you have a relationship, invest in it. Nurture it. Never take it for granted. When customers are in a long-term relationship with a provider they trust who is doing a good job at fair prices, it's going to be hard for anyone else to get them to switch horses. That's the provider you want to be.

What Making the Sale Really Means

At LMG, when we close a deal, we've made a commitment. The contract might be pages of itemized equipment and schedules, but what we're really saying is this: "You, the customer, are the most important priority in the world to us. We're going to do as we say and say as we do. You can rest assured that we have done everything humanly possible to make sure your event will go as you want, and if anything fails, we have a plan to deal with it."

When I make a sales presentation and we get the business, I believe to the core of my being that we are helping the customer. We're going to take care of them and do the best possible job. I'm not trying to just get the business for the sake of having the business, I want to help them. I want to elevate the quality of their events. I want to help them do things they haven't done before. And whether it's on a conscious or subconscious level, they know that.

When I'm the Buyer

Even though LMG has a purchasing department that handles most of the routine buying, I'm still involved in major purchases. My relationships with most of our suppliers go back to the early days of the company. I like to negotiate the major transactions for two main reasons: One, I enjoy the art of the deal, and two, I want to make sure we receive optimum pricing.

In its purest form, when you're buying something, the law of supply and demand is in force. But there's still almost always the opportunity for negotiation. A lot of people, sometimes even savvy businesspeople, don't know how to capitalize on that negotiation opportunity. They aren't willing to test the waters with some simple questions, such as:

Can I get a deal on this?

Are there any sales or specials?

Do you have any B stock (open boxes or equipment that has been used as a demo)?

Asking the right questions is the first step in testing the negotiating waters, of getting a sense of whether you can get a lower price or better terms. If you don't throw any bait in the water, you definitely won't catch any fish. They're not going to fly out of the ocean, jump on your hook, and say, "I'm here, take me." And suppliers aren't going to voluntarily sweeten their deal when you haven't asked for it. So ask, even if you're not comfortable doing it. After you ask the first time and it produces a positive results, you'll keep on asking.

Purchasing is more art than science. Sure, there's the "science" side where you're dealing with specs and numbers. But the negotiation side is an art.

Something my friend John Gardner (I'll tell you more about him in Chapter 9) taught me many years ago was: Don't negotiate on price until you're ready to buy. Sellers are never going to give you the best price until the only thing you have left to do is determine the price and close the deal.

Simply telling the seller you want a better price isn't enough. First, you have to define what a better price is. Second, the seller needs to know that you have options, and you may have to explain what your alternatives are. That's why you need to know what other products could meet your needs and what other manufacturers are selling comparable products for. Most manufacturers already know that already, and they know that unless their product is special or truly unique, they're going to have to get to a certain price point to make the sale. If the product you're negotiating can be rented instead of purchased and that's an option you'd consider, you may want to factor that into your negotiations.

When a manufacturer builds a widget I want and they're not willing to negotiate on price, a strategy I often use is to find another manufacturer who builds a similar product that will work for my needs and costs less. Before I made a final decision, I'll go back to the first manufacturer and say, "I want to buy your product. But I can buy something similar that will serve my purpose from another company and get a much better deal. If you don't want to sell your product to me at [I name a specific price], that's what I'm going to do." Then they have the option of losing the business or giving me the price I want to pay.

When you ask for a better deal, it becomes a business decision on the seller's part whether to take your offer or not, based on the pros and cons of the deal. Sometimes they'll say yes, sometimes they won't. You need to be prepared with a real, workable backup plan if the seller says no.

Giving your preferred source a final offer and a clear statement of what you'll do if they say no is a simple and honest negotiating technique. In fact, I wish our customers would use it with us. If they would say, "I'll pay you this much if you want the show, and if you don't, I'll use someone else," and I could say "yes" and get the business or "no" and lose the business, it would be great. The key here is keeping it honest. Don't claim to have an alternative source at a great price if you don't. You'll probably get caught and your negotiating credibility will be gone.

Most sales training courses spend a lot of time stressing how important it is for salespeople to know their customers. When you're the customer, it's equally important for you to know as much as you can about your suppliers. The more you know, the easier it will be for you to negotiate the best deal. Here's a great example of that concept in action:

We buy a lot of equipment from several Asian manufacturers. One of the ways these companies measure their performance is on forecasting production. At the end of each month, they want their warehouses to be empty—and over the years, that's gotten us some incredible deals because they'd rather sell product at a deep discount than have it left in their warehouse. Even as I share this, I want to stress that the best deal in the world is only the best deal if you can deploy the capital and have it produce a return. Buying something you can't capitalize just to get a good deal is actually a bad deal.

In contrast, we buy from a European manufacturer that is very rigid on price. There's absolutely no negotiating; if we want their products, we pay their asking price. When you're facing a seller like that and you want their product, find out if they're willing to negotiate on the terms or on some other aspect of the deal.

> *The more you know about your suppliers and their competitors, the easier it will be for you to negotiate the best deal.*

Here's another example of how understanding your suppliers works to your advantage: Manufacturers typically offer volume discounts and some offer discounts based on the status of the customer (which may also be tied to volume). It's common to assume that you'll always get the best price buying direct from the manufacturer, but that's not always the case. Years ago, I realized that I could get better prices on some equipment buying from other companies instead of direct from the manufacturer because those companies were buying in much larger quantities, getting substantial discounts, and passing those savings along to their customers.

In our industry, the standard discount manufacturers give to rental companies is usually nominal because the volume rarely justifies a significant price reduction. The discounts for resellers are generally higher because resellers tend to buy greater volume. We recognized that we could get greater discounts on almost everything we bought if, in addition to our live event business, we had a department that would sell and install the equipment. That's when LMG Systems Integration was born. That division installs permanent audiovisual systems for markets such as corporate, healthcare, education, emergency operations centers, and houses of worship. Those permanent installations use much of the same equipment, technology, and expertise as the live events, so the new division was compatible with our core business. It increased our overall revenue and reduced our costs to purchase rental equipment.

On a per item basis, the margins in rental are typically going to be higher than in a permanent installation. For live events, we buy the item once and rent it multiple times. For fixed installations, we buy the item, mark it up, and sell it one time. But those fixed installation purchases have the potential to boost our overall volume to the point that we earn a greater discount even on the rental equipment, and that puts us in a more advantageous market position overall. However, there are still some things we buy through distributors rather than direct from manufacturers because that's how we get the best price.

It all comes down to this: No one wants to lose. Your suppliers don't want to lose. Their competitors don't want to lose. And you certainly don't want to lose. Learn to leverage that and use strong negotiating techniques to produce the best result.

Special Circumstances

There will be times you're taking a risk and you'll ask your suppliers to share in the risk by offering favorable pricing, such as when you're entering a new market or offering a new service. If we're doing something that could ultimately mean more business for our suppliers by developing a market that hadn't previously existed, it's to their benefit to offer us special pricing and support. I tell them what we're doing and give them a chance to be a part of it. And if they agree, we will promote their products as part of our solution, so they get advertising and marketing on the back end for what we're doing.

More than Price

My goal is to get the best price on everything I buy. By "best," I mean that optimal combination of cost and value. If I'm going to offer the best price to my customers, I have to get the best price from my suppliers.

In any discussion of negotiating, it's easy to focus on

price, but price isn't the only issue. It's important and you never want to pay more than you have to for what you're getting, but there's more to the best price than beating on the seller to see how low they'll go. You have to get the quality you need.

We rarely overpay when we're buying, which is one of the reasons we have been consistently profitable for more than 30 years. But we don't buy junk, either. We refuse to risk failing our customers by using substandard equipment. When we're on the selling side of the table, we don't sell price, we sell value. If you want what we do, if you want to be able to sleep at night, you're going to hire us even though we're rarely going to be the low cost provider.

Regardless of which side of the negotiating table you're on, there's a psychology to pricing you need to understand. If you're the buyer and you make an offer that's accepted without discussion, did you offer too much? If you're the seller and you name a price the buyer immediately accepts, are you selling too low? In most cases, the answer to both questions is yes. And only experience and educating yourself will help you get to the point where that doesn't happen.

Another important negotiating tip is that you need to have the ability to close. You've got to have the cash or the financing ready to go so that you don't have to delay closing by getting approvals. Our suppliers know that when I say, "We have a deal," it's done and they're going to get paid. They don't want to throw out a great price and then have to wait days, weeks, or even months to find out if they're going to get the sale.

Finally, when you're negotiating, be firm but don't be a bully. Nobody likes a bully and bullying is not the way to build relationships. The best negotiations are accomplished without friction.

Working Things Out

In Chapter 3, I mentioned the importance of developing good habits as early as possible. When I was in my late 20s, I found the gym—and going to the gym regularly is a really good habit. Of course, exercise is good for your health. It keeps your body in shape and, for many people, it's a way to manage stress.

When I developed the gym habit, I discovered another benefit. I found myself talking to people and building business relationships with them. I've met people at the gym that I probably would not have met otherwise. I've met doctors, lawyers, corporate executives, and business owners in all kinds of industries. We've developed relationships, shared connections, and done each other favors outside the gym. And it's worth mentioning that I met my wife at the gym, so you can understand why I say the gym is my happy place.

I try to go at the same time (usually in the morning) on the same days of the week because it's easier to keep it in my schedule and I see the same people so we have a chance to get to know each other. I have memberships in two different gyms because the facilities have different machines. A bonus of maintaining two memberships is that I have the opportunity to meet twice as many people.

There are plenty of things you can do to exercise and stay in shape, but in my experience, nothing gives you greater returns than a gym membership. Sign up for trials at a couple of different gyms and see how you like them. Then pick one or two that will meet your personal needs while expanding your business horizons at the same time.

Persuade, Manipulate, or Command?

It's important to make the distinction between persuading, manipulating, and commanding whether it's in a sales, leadership, or other relationship situation.

Persuasion is stronger because it's based on integrity and honesty, and it builds on mutual self-interest. By finding the right buttons and pushing them, you get people to see things your way, take a particular action, or follow a certain path. You show people the wisdom of getting into your boat and all of a sudden you're all paddling in the same direction.

Manipulation is a lot like playing a game where you make up the rules as you go along to get the outcome you want by whatever means necessary. Your focus is on the immediate and short-term situation, not a long-term buy-in that works to everyone's benefit.

When you command, you're effectively functioning as a dictator. You may have the power, either because you're the boss or a customer who is the decision-maker, and you may get what you want in the short-term. But it won't last. Think about the last time you were ordered to do something. Even if it was a good idea and if you were willing to do it anyway, you probably resented the approach. And it almost certainly had a negative impact on your overall performance.

When you persuade, it sticks. It gets everybody on the same team, working together, building momentum. When you manipulate or dictate, you'll often end up with buyer's remorse, a change of heart, or a general sense of distrust.

Does it take more effort to persuade? Sometimes, but not always. If both will get you what you want, is it worth it to persuade rather than manipulate? Yes. Always. Every time.

Chapter Eight

What You Can Learn from Chess

If you play chess, you know it mirrors life in many respects. I used to play chess with my maternal grandfather, Sam Tabachnick, who loaned me the money to start LMG. He was a unique character, about five feet tall, as bald as ET. He had a fabric store in Brooklyn. When he shook your hand, he would feel your skin. If your skin was smooth, he'd say, "Ah, a thinker!" and if it was rough and calloused, he'd say, "Ah, you're a worker!" He was an entrepreneur and one of those people who would argue with you until you capitulated. I think I have a lot of his DNA.

My grandfather used chess as a way to teach me about strategy. He would say to me, "Just suppose I move this piece here, what are you going to do?" And I would think it through and figure out what I would have to do to win, considering all the possible things my opponent could do and how I would respond.

Running a business is like playing chess every day. We have to evaluate internal forces, external forces, what our opponents are doing, what we have to do to win, what's an acceptable loss. We have to understand strategies and know how to keep our plan to win moving forward even as we deal with unexpected moves from our opponents. We have to stay nimble, make good decisions quickly, and be able to recover from mistakes. I haven't found any single way to learn all of that better than by playing chess.

Bend so You Won't Break

As you navigate the ever-changing landscape of business, it's important to stay flexible. By flexible, I don't mean relative or ambiguous, I mean being willing to grow, learn, and change when necessary. In my experience, rigid people tend to be arrogant and self-righteous, and they rarely achieve notable success. More important, they're not happy. By contrast, flexible people can roll with the punches, adjust their course when necessary, and have a much more positive outlook in general. Using the chess analogy, if your opponent surprises you with a move that affects your strategy, you don't just give up. You reevaluate the situation and figure out what you need to change so you can win. And you remember what happened for the next game. Of course, when it comes to your vision, your commitment to excellence, your integrity, don't yield. But even the sharpest visionary can't see everything, so be flexible on the details and the path you'll take to get where you want to go.

Here's a classic example of flexibility in action: Regardless of how much planning and preparation you do, the live event business is full of surprises. I remember doing a show at Disney involving President George H. W. Bush and his Points of Light. It was going to be broadcast on one of the major network morning shows, and I had to be on site in the middle of the night to set up the teleprompter so Disney's then-CEO Michael Eisner could rehearse. The show was scheduled to be outside but had to be moved indoors at the last minute due to weather. For most events, this would have been a fairly routine thing of implementing the backup plan that's always part of an outdoor event. That plan is usually pretty simple—just move things inside. But this wasn't an ordinary event—this was a big deal with the sitting President of the United States and the chief executive officer of one of the largest and most recognizable entertainment companies in the world (with all of the related security, equipment, and support staff) appearing live on a national network television broadcast. There were a lot more moving parts and people to work around, but we got it done. And the audience never knew.

While building LMG and creating Entertainment Technology Partners, I've faced plenty of challenges—large and small, some I was able to anticipate, some I didn't see coming, and some were the direct result of mistakes I made.

What's important is that I've learned from most of these situations. I'm very much a historian. My philosophy is to learn from my experiences. If something goes well, we do it again—better, if possible. If something doesn't go well, we figure out what we can do differently next time. History has a way of repeating itself. If you ignore history, you'll see the same things happen over and over. Those of us who have seen the value of making changes as a result of history are able to produce different results in the future.

Lose a Battle, Win the War

There are times when you have to take a hit—and sometimes it's a pretty big hit—to keep a customer and protect your reputation. In chess, it's when you sacrifice a piece to advance your position. And it won't always be because of something you did wrong.

On any particular show, when our choice is to make money and do a poor job or lose money and do what we promised the customer, we'll lose money. I'd rather preserve our reputation and customer relationships than deliver less than we promised. In any business, if you're playing for the long haul, you might have to take it on the chin occasionally even when you're right. I value the relationships we've built over the years. Preserving them is not just a matter of personal pride, it's practical because in most cases, it costs more to acquire a new customer than it does to keep one you have happy. You can lose a few battles and still win the war.

There are, however, exceptions. In our industry—as I'm sure is the case in most industries—there are some clients that just aren't worth it. For example, they complain loudly because some minor thing isn't perfect just to get a reduction on their bill. Or they're hostile and rude to our people. We're used to demanding customers and we love challenges, but we don't want to work with customers who don't treat our people with respect. Not every company that reflects your market profile is going to be a good customer for you. There will be times when you are not the right fit for a customer or the customer isn't the right fit for you. It could be for a lot of reasons, ranging from minor to major. Just accept that there are companies out there that you don't want to work with either as a customer or a supplier because they take a different approach or value different things, and it might be successful for them but it won't be successful for you. Ideally you'll see this before you begin a relationship with them, but if you don't, your best strategy is to take steps to gracefully end the relationship without burning any bridges as soon as you realize the conflict. If you don't, you might win a few battles, but you'll ultimately lose the war.

Maintain Perspective on Problems

Problems happen, so deal with them. Equipment will fail. Deliveries won't be on schedule. Workers won't show. Customers will be unreasonable. Vendors will make mistakes. And so on.

If nobody died as a result of the problem, don't waste time and energy getting all worked up over it, just deal with it. It's important that we do our jobs the best we can, but most of us aren't doing brain surgery. Keep things in perspective or problems will drive you crazy. That you had a problem doesn't mean you've failed. Instead, that you had a problem and you resolved it should be counted as a success or a save.

In life, there is a circle of control, where we can control what's happening, and a circle of concern, where we are going to feel the impact of what's happening but we can't control it. I've learned to accept the things that are out of my control and just deal with the circumstances those things create.

In our business, getting the equipment to an event on time is critical. So it's within my circle of control to set policies that dictate how we choose transportation companies and schedule shipments. But sometimes trucks are going to be late because of mechanical or weather problems or for some other unavoidable reason. That's out of my control but in my circle of concern. I don't worry about what I can't control— that's a total waste of time. But I know there will be times when I'm going to have to deal with results of situations I couldn't control.

Have a Plan but Stay Flexible

Sometimes I refer to my planned business meetings as those moments between the interruptions of my day. Humor aside, it's important to end each day with the feeling that you achieved your goals for the day. The only way to do that is to start the day with a list of what you want to accomplish—and you have to write it down, don't try to keep it in your head. I keep my list on my calendar and I refer to it throughout the day so that I stay on track.

There are times when I have very few things on my calendar but I get overwhelmed by things that weren't scheduled. You have to be prepared for the unexpected. Our industry is particularly fluid. It has so many moving parts, so many places where a small glitch can snowball into a huge failure, and that makes it hard for people who are extremely structured and regimented to function. But if you're an owner, executive, or senior manager in any industry, you must be comfortable being reactive as well as proactive. You have to be able to solve problems in real time.

Be in charge of your time. Start your day with a plan and work the plan. Focus on the task at hand and—except in the case of an emergency—don't let yourself be distracted until that job is done. Be prepared to deviate from your plan if circumstances demand it, but make punctuality a priority. Don't keep others waiting—it's inconsiderate, disrespectful, and an expensive waste of time. And don't mistake being busy with being productive. Be sure what you're doing is actually generating results.

At the end of each day, if you have things you didn't finish, you have to decide if you can move them to another day's plan or if you need to keep at it until you get it done, no matter how long you have to work. There will always be more to do than there is time in the day.

Finding a system that works for you to keep you on time, on target, accomplishing your goals each day is imperative. If you don't start the day with goals, you won't know if you accomplished what you needed to when the day is over.

Expect an Attack

The more successful you become, the bigger your exposure to attack is. You worked hard to climb to the top of the mountain; there are plenty of people who want to be where you are but they don't want to work as hard as you did to get there. Much like you protect your key pieces when you're playing chess, you need systems and processes in place to protect your company and even you and your family personally from attacks.

As you run your business and interact with people in various situations and at various levels, there will be people who feel either that you didn't treat them fairly or that for some reason you owe them something. Sometimes those people will take any opportunity to poke at you. It's sad, but there are people who take joy in watching others get hurt.

There are plenty of resources out there to help you formulate plans to shield your company, yourself, and your family from virtual and real-world attacks. Don't wait until something happens to put your plans in place.

Take Time to Reflect

For the first 20 years that LMG was in business, I did absolutely no reflecting. Zero. I was a horse with blinders on, running at warp speed. I didn't look back at all.

I've learned that taking time to reflect on the past is good. There is tremendous value in remembering where you started, comparing it with where you are, and appreciating what you had to do to get there. I don't have any regrets, but I recognize that I probably should have done more reflection and analysis in the earlier stages.

Technology has had such a huge impact on our industry. It can be very nostalgic to remember when cameras were huge, when we recorded on videotape, when everything was done manually. But the importance of reflection goes beyond that. It reinforces our values. It helps us figure out what worked and what didn't so we can make good choices for the future. It's much easier to figure out where you're going and how you're going to get there if you remember where you came from.

Conquer Your World

Part of building a company is conquering the obstacles, creating something, and making it grow. In business, you can grow organically and through acquisitions. For much of its first three decades, LMG grew organically. We did more business and got bigger. While we've expanded to other cities as part of our growth plan, it doesn't make sense for us to open our own facility in every city in the world where we'd like to have a presence. What makes sense is for us to add acquisitions to our growth strategy. That logic was a big driver of the creation of Entertainment Technology Partners (ETP), which is now LMG's parent company.

We have to continue to grow to maintain our market share. If we're not growing, we're shrinking—and that's unacceptable to me. Nothing is standing still in this world. If you're in a place where you aren't growing but you've accepted the status quo and think it's good enough, I've got news for you: You're losing market share and you're shrinking, because though you may not be growing, your competitors are.

Conquer your world. Go for checkmate.

Chapter Nine

What to do with an Opportunity that isn't Part of the Plan

We all have stories about the one that got away, whether the "one" was a job, a business venture, a romance, or just a fish. Opportunities you weren't expecting are going to pop up and you'll either be ready to take advantage of them or you'll watch them pass you by. Your boat could be sailing smoothly in one direction and you may have to change course to chase the surprise opportunity. Don't automatically decide not to change course just because the new opportunity wasn't in the plan.

As I discussed in Chapter 7, be flexible. Be prepared to either take advantage of a new opportunity or make a conscious decision not to. The point is that your choice must be deliberate, not accidental.

When I started LMG, my plan was to grow our inventory by purchasing new and used equipment that was already functioning and in good condition. During our second year in operation, Tom Amason (you'll recall that he was my first customer; he was the hotel AV manager who rented my first projector) moved to Texas to take a job with the world's largest audiovisual equipment provider. That company had a bunch of Aquastar projectors, just like my first one, and they used to fail regularly. Tom told me that because they couldn't keep them working, they had decided to just get rid of them. Buying broken equipment wasn't part of my plan, but I immediately saw an opportunity.

As it happens, the Aquastar factory and repair facility was in Titusville, Florida, which is a short drive from Orlando. I had the idea of buying the broken units, getting them repaired, and then renting them back to Tom's company and other customers. At the time, Aquastars cost around $15,000 new. I initially bought six or eight of them for $500 each, got them fixed, and put them into my rental inventory at the rate of $500 a day. It only took one rental to recoup my investment and if the unit broke, it was fairly easy to get it repaired. For the next three years, I bought those broken projectors, got them repaired, and rented them out. It was a great deal all the way around. I solved a problem for Tom by taking these broken projectors off his hands and providing him with working units as he needed them, and I was making money.

Prompted by a Teleprompter

When LMG was just a year or two old, we were providing audiovisual equipment for an IBM event at one of the Disney hotels. I got a call from the teleprompter operator who needed a black and white monitor. When I took the monitor out to the site, I saw a teleprompter for the first time. I was fascinated with it and thought there would be value in being able to offer teleprompter services.

These days, most of us know what a teleprompter is and we're familiar with the angled screens we see in front of speakers at live events. Here's a little history: The first teleprompter was devised in the late 1940s as an alternative to handwritten cue cards for live television actors. It was a series of belts, pulleys, and a motor that turned a scroll of paper that displayed the actors' lines. It didn't take long for the first in-camera teleprompter to be developed. That machine projected the script directly in front of the lens so the on-screen talent could look into the camera and appear to be looking directly at the audience. After that, broadcast news operations began using teleprompters instead of the printed scripts anchors had held in their hands. During the 1952 presidential election, teleprompters were used by both parties at their conventions, and now they're standard at all types of shows and events.

In the early 1980s, teleprompter systems were computerized. That meant that instead of typing an entire speech or presentation at 19 characters per line on paper, ASCII text files could be imported into a computer and displayed on a monitor—no paper *and* you could edit the content on the fly. I decided LMG needed a computerized teleprompter system.

When I told my mom about it (remember, I was still in my teens, living at home), she offered to buy and operate the equipment and we would split the revenue. Operating a teleprompter was—and still is—one of those "not as easy as it looks" jobs. Our first show was for American Express at the Hilton Lake Buena Vista, and my mother was so stressed she thought she was going to have a heart attack. She never did another show.

But LMG was one of the few equipment providers in Central Florida that had teleprompters, so it was worth it to learn how to operate them myself and then find and train others on the equipment. It was my first step outside of the basic audiovisual products of cameras, projectors, and screens, but it wouldn't be my last.

Beyond the direct revenue, the teleprompter segment of the business turned out to be one of the best things that happened to me. In those early days, I was still hands-on, working as many of the shows as I could. So I not only made money from renting the equipment, I received the education from hearing the speakers who were using the teleprompters.

Why Can't You Open a Bar?

I met John Gardner at an auction when I was 16 and he was in his mid-20s. We were both bidding on an Advent television set, which was one of the most popular home projectors of the day. When the bid amount reached my maximum, I quit bidding. John dropped out about the same time, too, because the price was getting higher than the value of the item. But there was another Advent coming up and we were both looking at that one when I struck up a conversation with him by asking him why he was interested in that particular TV.

"I'm a disc jockey, we're about to provide entertainment services for a nightclub and I need a projector for the music videos," he said. He had just signed a contract with one of the big hotels in Lake Buena Vista and need additional equipment.

"This is not what you need," I told him. "I'm in the AV business, I can help you. You need an Aquastar."

He was skeptical and told me I looked like a high school student, which I was. But he didn't have much money and didn't know much about the equipment, so instead of walking away, he asked, "What do you mean, you have an AV business?"

"I'll prove it to you," I said. I took him out to my car, my battered old Chevy Citation, and handed him my price sheet, which was a plain list of the equipment I had and the rental rates.

John looked at it and said, "Dude, this is just a sheet of paper."

I persisted. "I'm in the business. I can help you."

Later, John told me that he figured talking to me further wasn't too big of a risk because he didn't know anything about how to do what he wanted to do and even though I was young, I seemed to know what I was talking about (and I did).

We went back inside, both of us bid on the second Advent, but neither one of us got it. After the auction, I told him I had to go shoot my high school football game for our TV show "Proud to be a Patriot" but that I could take him on an after-hours tour of Storer Cablevision afterward. We agreed to meet at Storer later. While I was shooting the game, I began to have second thoughts about taking him inside the Storer facility. I was afraid I might get into trouble for it. So I waited in my car for him to get there and offered to take him to my house to show him my business. He accused me of wasting his time but agreed to follow me home.

My equipment was in the garage, in the bonus room above the garage, and in my bedroom (which was all the places my mom would allow me to use for storage). I showed him everything, explaining that I would buy these things at auction and rent them to local restaurants and bars for them to show Monday Night Football. This was 1984, before the development of the sports bars that are so popular today. Places would pay me to bring in my big screen TV sets and they would pick up the over-the-air broadcast signal for the game and people in the bar could watch it. I could buy an Advent TV set for $300 at auction and rent it for $100 a night. John listened to me and then he said, "So you have an AV business like a kid would have a lawn mowing business." That was a pretty accurate description of what I was doing at the time.

I knew of a place in Miami that had good deals on Aquastar projectors. I told John that I would rent him one of my Advent TVs on a temporary basis until he could get his own Aquastar. It ended up that I bought two and he bought one, and we drove down to South Florida together to pick them up.

We became good friends, in spite of the difference in our ages. We did things together and learned about each other's businesses. And years later, he was the best man at my wedding. But back to those early days: John's nightclub gig in the hotel was doing great—unfortunately, too great. He was playing new wave music and was attracting huge crowds. But it wasn't the right clientele for a hotel bar and the bar patrons were interfering with the hotel guests. After a year, they canceled his contract and kicked him out with only about a week's notice. When he told me, I asked what he was going to do.

"I'm going to try to get a job at a nightclub and DJ somewhere," he said. "I can do a new wave night because no one else is doing it."

I said, "What would happen if you opened your own nightclub?"

"It would be packed," he said, "but I can't open a nightclub, I don't have any money."

I assured him that he could indeed open a nightclub. Even then, I knew anything was possible. And it made sense, because he'd had his own mobile DJ business and he already owned all the sound and video equipment he needed; he just needed a place. I told him that I would contribute 25 percent of the cash he was able to come up with to get it started. I was 17—not even old enough to drink and I was advising my friend to open a nightclub and offering to invest in it with him. In retrospect, it seems a little crazy, but we didn't think so at the time.

He went looking for a location and found an old pizzeria on Orange Blossom Trail in Orlando that was vacant. But the owners had decided they were going to tear it down instead of renting it to another tenant. I asked him who the owners were and it turned out they lived next to my parents. I had known them for years. So when I asked if they'd reconsider their decision, they agreed because I was involved.

John managed to come up with $9,000 and I put in $3,000. We signed the lease on a Monday and opened for business on Friday. John came up with the name Faith in Physics. I wasn't old enough to get in as a customer, but I sat at the door that first night, collecting the cover charge. John was right when he said the club would be packed. He had built a following and his regular customers all showed up.

I didn't spend a lot of time at the nightclub because I was focusing on going to college and building LMG, but we still had a very effective and profitable partnership. John understood the entertainment side and I understood business. After a couple of years, we moved the nightclub downtown. We started out selling just beer and wine and eventually were able to get a full liquor license. We changed the name a couple of times, and John offered to buy me out in 1999 and I agreed. John still owns it; today, it's called Independent Bar or IBar. John also owns clubs in Austin and Houston and has built a multimillion-dollar business from that first little club we opened on a shoestring.

The two points of sharing this story are: One, John wasn't planning to open his own nightclub but when he saw the opportunity, he took advantage of it. Two, I truly don't understand the *why not* of anything I want to do. I only understand *why* and *how*. When you start believing it's impossible, it is. And when you believe something is possible, you can get it done one way or another.

Expand in the Direction of the Business

When it comes to planning the growth of a company, entrepreneurs need to be both visionary and reactionary. Steve Jobs was famous for relying on his intuition rather than market research. He once told *Business Week*, "A lot of times, people don't know what they want until you show it to them." While that approach worked for the charismatic Jobs and extremely innovative Apple products, it's not going to consistently work for most companies.

From LMG's early days, I've found that listening to our customers and paying close attention to the general state of our market is the best way to grow. In that respect, we let the market pull us. We figure out where the opportunities are likely to be and aim in that direction. At the same time, we are a primary resource for our customers when it comes to leading-edge show technology. We go beyond just giving them what they say they want; we make suggestions for things they may not have thought of that could make their events better. And before we suggest something, we need to know how it works. I've been known to cause our executive team some serious agita when I purchase new equipment before a customer asks for it—although most of the time, my intuition is on target.

And then there are the times when business opportunities will just fall in your lap. When that happens, take advantage of it.

Feed the Pipeline

Go after every piece of business as though it's the most important, most profitable job ever. You won't win every bid, but you should try. Even if you're not 100 percent sure you can do it, go for it anyway. That's how you grow. You have to keep tackling new opportunities that are bigger, better, and push your envelope. Remember that no one is going to build a skyscraper without having built a few one- and two-story buildings first.

A challenge common to our industry and many others is that most companies would be in serious trouble if they did win every bid because they wouldn't have the resources to handle the business. But you shouldn't decline to bid on a project just because you have other pending bids and you aren't sure which ones are going to get accepted. Go after them all—and if you get more business than you expected, good for you. Figure out how to handle it. That's the best kind of problem to have.

Expect and Capitalize on the Unexpected

LMG Touring was born out of an unexpected opportunity. It wasn't part of our business plan at the time, but because we understand the value in staying flexible, we were able to take a surprise request and grow it from a single tour to a thriving division with a client roster that includes some of the world's hottest superstars.

Years ago, we hired an audio engineer who had worked for Avril Lavigne as a front of house touring engineer. She hadn't toured for a while, but in 2007 she decided to go on the road and wanted him to join the tour. Because he was employed by LMG, he brought the opportunity to us and said the only way he would take the job with her was if he did it with our equipment and as our employee. We weren't looking to get into the touring business, but we quickly realized we'd found a parallel universe to our core business. Touring required much of the same gear that our show clients used, but it was packaged and charged for differently and the technicians lived on the road. After we did our first Avril Lavigne tour, we realized this was a market we could serve.

The way we got involved in that first Avril Lavigne tour was an exception to the way the touring industry typically operates in that the artist specifically wanted to work with one of our employees. We rarely work directly with the artists; while it happens, for the most part we're dealing with the production team that puts on the show. One of the reasons LMG remains a strong, growing company is due to our commitment to developing and maintaining relationships. But we didn't have relationships in the touring industry at the time, so we had to establish them. We did our research and began building relationships with those production teams. And no matter who the acts were or what size venue they were playing, we treated them all like they were the most important client in the world. As we developed our touring business, we realized that some of the smaller acts didn't get the same level of attention from the large touring companies that the major acts did. I believe in treating people the way I want to be treated and in giving them the respect they deserve. That philosophy has been one of the key elements that has driven our growth over the years.

As we began to gain new touring accounts, we realized something else: When a C act tour is over, the production manager moves on to the next tour, and it could be another C act, or it could be a B or even an A act. Because we took care of the production managers on the smaller tours, they came back to us for the bigger ones.

> *Treat all of your customers like each one is the most important customer in the world.*

A production manager told me about an experience he had calling a major trucking company for a quote for a single truck for a tour. That's not a big tour by industry standards, but it's important to the artist and the production company. The response he got was, "Are we bidding the tour or do we have the tour?" The question made it clear that the trucking company didn't feel like it had to work to win the business and the production manager felt like he wasn't an important enough customer to the trucking company. When he told me that story, he was comparing the attitude of that trucking company to our philosophy of believing we have to earn the business, we have to do it every day, with every show, and that keeps us on our toes.

The major difference between the corporate shows that are the core of our business and the touring industry is that the corporate shows are one-time events and touring shows are staged almost every night for three or four months. In the corporate arena, you've got one chance to do the show right. There are no do-overs. In the touring world, the shows get tweaked as the tour progresses. After the first show, you find ways to make it better. And if something doesn't go right on one show, it can be fixed for the next one.

The stakes for corporate events are much higher because the customer's goal is to make a major impression on the audience, whether it's communicating with shareholders, training and motivating sales reps, promoting products to customers, or whatever the meeting's purpose is. A tour is about an audience that's interested in listening to and buying music, and they're usually fans of the artist to start with so they tend to be far more forgiving if something isn't right.

We apply the same high standards to every show, whether it's a one-time major event, a convention, a superstar's tour, or the tour of a struggling performer just getting started. That's what distinguishes us from other touring companies and that's how we were able to turn a chance occurrence into a multimillion-dollar business unit.

The touring business is tough on people. It's not easy living on a bus, staying on the road for months at a time, getting out in a field in the middle of a rainy night to pull feeder cable through the mud. But there's nothing cooler than going backstage with a backstage pass and meeting the artists, getting house seats for the performance, and being part of an art form where you're adding the technology component.

While this is a sexy and (at least from the outside) glamorous business, it's important to note that this worked because the touring industry is compatible with our core event business. If an "opportunity" isn't compatible with your core business, it could divide your attention and your resources, confuse your customers, and have a negative impact on your reputation.

Is it Worth the Risk?

Nothing in this world is completely risk-free. If you're going to do great things, you have to take some risks. But you shouldn't take crazy, stupid risks—your risks should be carefully calculated.

One of the risks I take fairly often is investing in new technology before our customers ask for it. I don't want customers telling us they've heard about new technologies that might work for them; I want us to be the ones to say, "We've got this great new [whatever] that will be perfect for your next project."

This doesn't mean I buy every new gadget that comes along. I know how to look at something through the eyes of our customers and understand how they're likely to value it. And though I have made mistakes, I have a good track record for being right most of the time.

There will be times when you have to take risks to keep your customers happy. Often they won't know you're taking risks and if they did they probably wouldn't care. That doesn't matter, because when you do the job well, they'll keep coming back.

Sometimes what seems like a risk really isn't. When one of my customers was doing a show in Nigeria, he put the job out for bid. Every other company bid at least five times more than the customer's budget would allow. Our bid came in slightly under his budget. He figured the other companies didn't really want the job because they were afraid of losing their gear by shipping it to Nigeria. We understood the risk and we mitigated it with insurance. All of the gear was covered by customer-provided insurance so we were either going to get it back or get paid for it. To me it was simple. Why would we charge substantially more over our standard markups to ship equipment to Nigeria than we would to ship equipment to New York or Los Angeles? We made a nice profit on that show in Nigeria and they returned all the equipment in good condition except for a few small pieces (which is common) that were missing.

Make a Decision

Decision-making is sometimes an art and sometimes a science. One of the most important things successful people have in common is the ability to make decisions quickly. They don't worry about having *all* of the information, they don't overthink. They get enough data to evaluate the risks and rewards and then they decide and take action.

Not making a decision is a decision in itself—it's saying *no* in a drawn-out and potentially damaging way. Not deciding is actually a bad decision, and bad decisions tend to reinforce themselves with more bad decisions. You won't always make the right decision, but make one anyway.

I have strong instincts that are usually dead-on. I don't warm up to people and ideas—I either like them right away or I don't. Odds are, if you don't feel good about someone or something in the beginning, it's not going to get any better.

> *You won't always make the right decision,*
> *but make one anyway.*

Develop and learn to trust your intuition. Don't over-analyze and don't vacillate. That wastes time and can create missed opportunities because someone else will take action while you're thinking.

I'm known for making a decision about whether or not to hire someone in the first three minutes of an interview. I call it the vibe. But trusting the vibe is not just about people, it's about all situations—decisions to go after a particular piece of business, to move forward on a project, to make a purchase. The pace of business today is too fast for leisurely decisions. You make the best decision you can with the information you have on the day you have it. Once you've made the decision, move forward.

People who make good decisions are generally proud of them and willing to share them. That's a good gut check tool for the times when you aren't sure you're making the best choice. Do you feel comfortable telling others about your decision? If you don't, you might want to reconsider your plan.

Have I ever made decisions when I wasn't sure I was doing the right thing? Of course. There's no guarantee that you're going to have all the correct answers. All you'll know is that at the one point in time, based on the information you have, you figured out what to do to achieve the best possible outcome. There's nothing more you can do.

It's important to build a team of people you can trust to provide you with the information you need to make decisions—people who can do the research and analysis, people who have good resources. And if someone gives you information and it turns out to be wrong because they made a mistake, you have an opportunity for coaching.

Will all of your decisions be right? Probably not. But not making a decision is worse than making the wrong decision.

Condition yourself to always be prepared to recognize, evaluate, and seize opportunities. Of course, the smaller you are, the easier it is to move quickly to take advantage of unexpected situations. As you grow, it's important to maintain a high degree of nimbleness—to run your company like a speedboat, not an ocean liner. Remember, if you don't, someone else will.

Chapter Ten

It's Never the Wrong Time for the Right Thing

We're living in a far different world today than when I started LMG in 1984. Though times have changed, the formula for success hasn't. You have to have unique ideas for which there is market demand and you've got to work hard. Nothing is easy—if it was easy, everyone would do it.

As I've said, I don't understand *no*. People can be so quick to just say, "No, that can't be done," when the truth is they really just don't want to figure out how to get it done. I truly believe anything is possible. Your perspective on anything should not be why it won't work or why we can't do it, it should be how we're going to overcome obstacles and achieve our vision.

In my opinion, too many people are willing to reject the idea that anything is possible. It seems like they'd rather figure out why they can't do something than why they can. Those people will drag you down; don't let them do it. When you want to tackle something that might appear to be the equivalent of an average, non-athletic person climbing Mount Everest, refusing to accept *no* for an answer is an essential component of your success.

I'm a dreamer with a keen vision for what I think the future of technology and how it can be applied to my industry will be. And I won't accept no for an answer. I have a track record of pushing and pushing until I achieve incredible results, and then people say, "Wow, how did you do that?" I did it by believing it was possible and not taking no for answer.

It's Not About the Money

LMG and my other business investments have allowed me to make a lot of money and enjoy a lot of luxuries. But I don't want my success to be measured in dollars or expensive toys. A while back, someone who was traveling with me took a picture of me standing on the tarmac next to our corporate jet, talking to my pilot, with my sports car parked nearby. The person who took the picture thought it represented the epitome of success and he wanted to post it on social media. I said no because I don't want these material things to be the public measure of my success. What represents success to me is being the best in our industry, doing the best work, working with the best people, playing a key role in staging some of the biggest shows (and many smaller ones) that happen in around the world—even though very few people outside our business will ever know what we did. What represents success to me is being respected as a leader and an innovator in our industry.

To be a true success, you must be motivated by more than money. You can make money in any business, and if your goal is to make money, the business doesn't matter. But here's the problem with being motivated primarily or solely by money: After you have the money, what's going to continue to motivate you? How much money is enough? What will make you want to do bigger and better things?

Making money, or getting rich, is an outcome if a lot of good things happen—if you're in the right place at the right time, if you have the right formula, and if you work very hard. If you study what motivates very wealthy entrepreneurs, you'll find that money is way down on the list. One thing that's high on the list is that they're excited by finding a winning formula. They like being winners and money is just a byproduct of a winning formula.

My business—especially in the early days when I was operating the teleprompter—gave me the opportunity to work with some fascinating people. One of the best speeches I've ever heard was by Jerry Linenger, the American astronaut who spent 132 days on Mir, the Russian space station. His description of life in space was interesting, especially when he talked about dealing with a potentially catastrophic fire on board. But what really struck me was his message about the importance of balancing your work life and your home life and living fully every day because you don't know how many more days you're going to have.

I give my wife a lot of credit for helping me to appreciate the value of that. She's very family-centered, and before I knew her I was very work-centered. She taught me that nothing you can buy will ever be able to replace a great experience with your family. Things get old, they break, whatever. But memories last forever. And time with the people you love creates those priceless memories. As important as it is to work hard and stay focused on your business, it's equally important to make time for your family.

In 2005, I was honored to be the commencement speaker at Seminole State College (then Seminole Community College). I'd like to share with you part of what I told those graduates:

> *I challenge every one of you to dream big and believe your goals are possible. A passion for something lies inside each of you. Find it and realize how you can use your energy, enthusiasm, and passion to make a difference in the world.*
>
> *My company has a direct connection to most of the Central Florida colleges. We equip them to be what's referred to as smart classrooms. I couldn't have imagined this*

when I was a student here 20 years ago.

I am fortunate to have an incredible wife and three precious children who help me set my priorities every day. It takes a constant effort to find the balance between family and business. As you make your decisions about your future, remember to keep balance in your lives.

Never give up on yourself and your goals. The saying "quitters never win and winners never quit" is true. It won't be easy. But if you know what you want in life, with effort, commitment, and persistence, you can achieve it.

Thank you for letting me share this day with the class of 2005. Congratulations to the graduates and good luck as you start your new journey.

To you I say, thank you for letting me share my story and all the best on your journey. Remember, don't take no for an answer because anything is possible.

The Story in Pictures

The process of writing this book included taking a lot of trips in the "way-back machine" for the anecdotes that come together to tell the LMG story. In the process, I found pictures I'd like to share.

At my bar mitzvah with Grandpa Sam, who loaned me the $5,000 that I used to start LMG.

My high school video club. On the front row at left is Mark Grossman with Storer Cable; at center is Betty Fowler, who was in charge of the media center and who connected me with Big Les; and I'm on the back row at the right.

Photo by Bryn Alan Studio

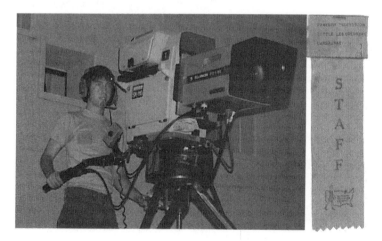

At the National Teenager Pageant. It was my first time operating a camera. The Hitachi SK110 was bigger than I was. My badge is on the right.

Working the 1984 Summer Olympics. I was operating an ADDA, a still image storage device.

At my desk in my first office.

With my parents at the open house celebrating the opening of our second office in 1985.

The exterior of our second office.

In front of our first building in 1993.

Backstage of the MONY show, Hyatt Grand Cypress, 1993.

At the Headdress Ball, a fundraiser for the
Hope & Help Center, with my wife, Julie.

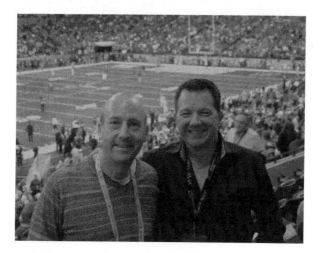

At Super Bowl XLVI in Indianapolis with Chuck
Whittall. LMG was doing the halftime show.

With Penn and Teller at a show for Northern Telecom in Orlando.

With the band The Fray. Craig Mitchell, our Director of Touring, is third from right.

Accepting the Chuck Hummer III Visionary
Award at the Headdress Ball in 2013.

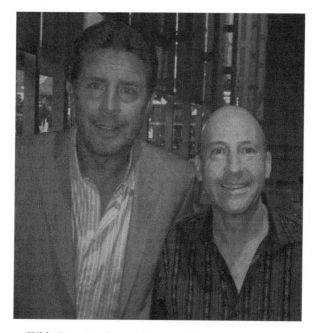

With Dan Marino at the AARP show celebrating
his 50th birthday.

At the Radio City Music Hall
Spring Spectacular 2015

With my friend John Gardner.

Our first Avril Lavigne tour in Tampa.

Train Tour 2014; The Script also performed.

LMG Orlando Headquarters

LMG Las Vegas office at ground level and from the air

LMG Nashville office

LMG Dallas office

LMG Detroit office

LMG Tampa office

30-in-30: We participated in The Color Run, an event designed to promote healthiness and happiness.

30-in-30: LMG donated gear to the 2014 Seminole State College's Dream Gala, which funds scholarships and other programs at the college.

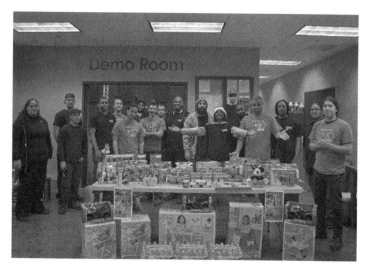

30-in-30: Our Las Vegas office collected donations for Help of Southern Nevada, a local agency that serves the poor, homeless, and those in crisis.

30-in-30: We donated 30 bags to Hi-5 Kids Pack, a program of the Second Harvest Food Bank of Central Florida that provides nutritious meals to needy children for weekends when they do not have access to school cafeterias.

30-in-30: We donated food to the Second Harvest Food Bank of Central Florida

30-in-30: Our Nashville office donated to Room in the Inn, an organization that provides shelter and other services to homeless people.

Acknowledgements

Credit for a book like this one goes beyond writing and producing the book itself to everyone who helped make the story possible, because without the story, there would be no book.

I'd like to begin by thanking my wife and three children for their unconditional love and immense patience. They regularly remind me of the importance of work-life balance, and every day they help make me a better person. I'd also like to thank my parents and my sisters whose support and enthusiasm has been unwavering.

Next, I'd like to thank all of the people—employees, suppliers, customers, performers, audiences—who contributed to our success in so many ways from the very beginning.

My gratitude for my executive team and the professionals (attorneys, accountants, and other advisors) who have guided me over the years is boundless. Of course, I appreciate every one of our team members. They are essential to our success.

The key people within LMG that I want to specifically acknowledge include: Stacy Teal, my assistant who helps me get it all done; Dave John, our Chief Operating Officer, who runs the company on a day-to-day basis; Rick Perry, our Chief Financial Officer; Steve Campbell, Vice President of Live Events; and Neil Morrison, Vice President of Technology.

I also need to mention John Gardner, Paul LaBruyere, and Chuck Whittall—my appreciation of their friendship is beyond measure.

And finally, Jacquelyn Lynn, whose writing and production skills helped me take an idea and turn it into a book.

We've shared an amazing journey and we still have a long way to go.

Les M. Goldberg

About Les. M Goldberg

Les M. Goldberg's professional titles include founder, chief executive officer, and president, but a more accurate description is that he is the driving force behind one of the entertainment technology services industry's leading players.

He started LMG in 1984 at the age of 17 with a $5,000 loan from his grandfather. LMG has grown from a small video equipment rental operation to a global leader in show technology, touring, and systems integration.

In 2014, Les created Entertainment Technology Partners (ETP), a parent company to a collection of exception brands in the industry. ETP's first acquisition was LMG. Under his guidance, the company is implementing a strategic acquisition plan that will support its brands as they take their performance to ever-higher levels.

In addition to being a business powerhouse, Les is a devoted family man. He makes his home in Orlando with his wife and their three children.

Connect with Les M. Goldberg

Visit Les's website, read his blog:
www.LesMGoldberg.com

Connect with Les on LinkedIn:
www.linkedin.com/in/lesmgoldberg

Follow Les on Twitter
www.twitter.com/LES_GOLDBERG

Invite Les M. Goldberg to Speak at Your Next Event

Beyond his passion for his own business, Les is passionate about entrepreneurship and enjoys sharing his expertise with a variety of audiences ranging from business students to corporate executives. To invite him to speak at your next event, please contact: admin@lesgoldberg.com.

ENTERTAINMENT
TECHNOLOGY PARTNERS

Entertainment Technology Partners (ETP) is the parent company to a collection of exceptional brands in the live event and entertainment technology services industry. Our shared philosophy embraces a distinctive approach to quality, service, and support.

We are integrated industry leaders driven by client relationships and focused on the goal of building and growing business. We're relentlessly looking for new and innovative ways to do it, be it a new technology or a more efficient way to better serve our customers.

ETP provides the platform to facilitate growth through strategic alliances, expanded assets, value creation and geographic reach. Our markets include corporate events and conventions, concert tours, fixed installations, theater, television and film, and special events.

To learn more about ETP, please visit us online at ETP.net or email info@ETP.net.

More Praise for *Don't Take No for an Answer* from Amazon.com Reader Reviews

Even if you are not in this crazy business of AV, you'll find countless examples of how drive, passion and a desire to provide the best to your clients can take you beyond your wildest dreams of success.

Great book for aspiring entrepreneurs or those just looking to find their way in the world of business. Les Goldberg's core values are rooted in his belief that success comes from following our passion. Do what you love to do, have fun, work hard, remain ethical and treat those around you with respect and dignity, and you are on the way to building your own successful career. Not all of us will end up flying in private jets and hanging out with famous people, but the down-to-earth message in this book is useful to anyone who wants to improve their game.

[Les Goldberg's] drive, passion and commitment should be admired and he makes me want to push myself harder to see how far I can go.

Made in the USA
Columbia, SC
01 January 2019